Author's Guide to

MARKETING

WITH TEETH

Author's Guide to

MARKETING
WITH TEETH

MICHAEL KNOST

SEVENTH STAR PRESS

Cover art: Michael Knost

Cover art in this book copyright © 2015 Enggar Adirasa & Seventh Star
Press, LLC.

Published by Seventh Star Press, LLC.

ISBN Number:

Seventh Star Press
www.seventhstarpress.com
info@seventhstarpress.com

Printed in the United States of America

First Edition

"To everyone who purchased a book out of pity when I was struggling at a lonely book signing."

INTRODUCTION

Let's be honest, the best marketing plan you can have is to write the best book you can. Because, no matter how hard you market your book, if it is not a good book, all you will do is increase a consensus that you are not a good writer. However, if your book is fantastic, then your marketing efforts will pay off with future dividends.

Let's face it, word-of-mouth is going to be the best marketing aspect that can work for you. However, word-of-mouth can be good or bad. If you have written a good book, then word-of-mouth can help sell more books than any other marketing efforts you can implement. If you've written a bad book, then word-of-mouth can destroy your name brand.

So, this book is working under the assumption that your book is fantastic.

Within these pages, you will find a tremendous amount of marketing ideas. I have worked in the marketing field for almost thirty years now, much of that time spent as general manager or sales manager of radio stations. I have also worked in advertising for newspaper and television. And, I have also worked as marketing director for some very big companies, seeing the other side, where I've bought advertising from just about every medium you can think about.

I have worked with small budgets up to annual budgets of over five million, and I have seen just about everything there is to see. However, I'm not going to try to tell you and I know it all. Because I don't. Marketing is not a static thing. It is ever changing, always evolving. And if anyone ever tells you that they have the marketing thing down pat, you can rest assured they are either lying or they are crazy.

What you are about to read is a culmination of a number of things. Over the years I have written a lot of articles, essays, and columns touching on the subject of marketing. In fact, I currently write a monthly column for the HWA (Horror Writers Association) newsletter. Many of the articles I have written over the years are included in this book. However, the majority of the content was written specifically for this book. I bring this up simply because I want you, the reader, to know why it reads in a certain way.

Think of this as a collection of pieces regarding marketing. Don't think of it as something that is going to have a continuity of a storyline with a beginning, middle, and end. The subject matter ranges from many topics, so don't expect connected narrative with an organic flow. Again, Think of this as a collection of ideas. I have, however, attempted to put everything in an order that makes sense.

And I should point out that some of the information I offer shows up several times in various places. Again, this is because it was written in separate articles at different times. However, the reason I left them in all the locations is the thing I mention multiple times are very important and I want you to recognize that.

Also, I want to point out that many of the articles may lean heavily toward the marketing or advertising side, with examples that may not always focus solely on authors or books. This is because I am hoping to impart universal marketing knowledge and experience so you understand the why. It is my hope, that as a reader, you can take this raw knowledge and apply it as an author in order to sell more books.

Michael Knost
August 9, 2015

LET'S GO FISHING

"I see a ton of people who say they've figured marketing out, but they're either selling their services or basing it on anecdotes 'I did this and it seemed to work.' Is there any actual data that authors can access on what helps and how much (cost-benefit analysis, etc.)?"
— Ken. Cranston, RI.

First of all, anyone who says they've got this marketing stuff figured out is either lying or insane. I mean, think about it, marketing is not a static thing—it's changing and evolving by the minute. What worked six months ago may not work today.

Which is why basing results on trial and error is the only way to find the sweet spot, and to then find the next sweet spot. So, the idea of, "I did this and it seemed to work" is the best approach one has when trying to wrap one's brain around this whole marketing thing.

For instance, let's think about marketing for automobiles. Industry professionals follow trial and error to the hilt. If something doesn't work, move on to something else. It's like bass fishing. Before you go out on the boat, you make sure your tackle box is bursting at the seams with a variety of lures, baits, and things to ensure success.

There are several types of lures when bass fishing. You

have crankbaits, spinnerbaits, plastics, tubes, topwaters, and jigs. Crankbaits and spinner baits allow you to cover a lot of water, and work best in light vegetation and rocky bottoms. Jigs give you a very accurate feel on the line, and are one of the most effective lures when used with a pork rind trailer.

Topwaters are best in very shallow water, or in areas that are covered in surface vegetation, such as lily pads. Plastics are the most versatile. They can be fished weighted or weightless. Floating plastics can be used just like a topwater, and any type of plastic can be fished weedless to allow fishing in extremely heavy vegetation.

And then there is the matter of color. Let's say you have a specific plastic worm that does well for you. If the fish are biting when you have a white one on the hook, and then they stop biting after a while, just changing to an orange worm of the same shape and size could get the fish biting again.

And don't forget, you can always use live bait. I don't need to go through all the types you could use, but you know there are a ton of options.

This is why having many options in your tackle box is imperative. After all, marketing is a trial and error thing. In fact, many businesses try to track where their results come from in marketing, but it is a very difficult thing to attempt.

Some businesses use multiple phone numbers in their marketing efforts. One specific phone number (customers call) is used only in radio (or one specific radio station), another number is used only in newspaper ads, and another number shows up only in television ads. The receptionist can keep track of the number of calls with each phone number, letting the business owner know which aspect of the marketing industry is a better lure for the moment.

Now, tracking can even be drilled down further by tracking calls that come from radio station X. You note how many calls came from the number, and you can also show how many sales you made from all those calls. It's like counting seven fish you caught with a specific lure after getting dozens of bites.

As far as actual available data, unfortunately there is nothing like that accessible. I'm sure it exists. I'm sure the major houses spend quite a bit of money producing data (from trial and error) that will give them a temperature of the water at that moment. However, they are not going to share that information.

This is why creating your own is so important. But, here's the thing: if you don't take the time to measure for yourself, you're never going to know the water's temperature. And that means you have to be on the water a lot. That means you have to cast the line out as many times as possible. Think about it, if you go out to the lake and cast your line only three times, you will only have three chances to reel one in. The more times you throw the line out, the more chances you have of reeling more in.

The angler searches for structure and cover, as this is where schools of fish mill about. Fallen trees, rock formations, weeds, and other items that can be a safe haven, are all ideal places to start. So, as an author hoping to catch readers, where are their structures and cover? Conventions, book festivals, libraries, and bookstores are only a few that come to mind.

I often visit bookstores as I have the addiction myself. I always try to chat with the managers and other personnel about what is selling and what is not. I'm curious how many titles of certain genres they've moved in the past month. I want to know what average sales of their end-cap displays are, and how much more percentagewise they are selling in comparison to books from the shelves. These folks love to talk about these numbers as much as I do.

So, the best advice I can give you is to fill your tacklebox with as much diverse marketing aspects as you can, and be prepared to change things up when the temperature drops, or the color of the water changes, or the structure is damaged or moved.

It's all about trial and error, but more important, as I mentioned earlier, it's about casting the line out as much as possible. The more lines you cast, the more chances you have for sales. So, keep casting. Make adjustments when needed. Study the conditions and adapt as quickly as possible. And take notes.

An angler may remember a chartreuse plastic worm worked really well in cold conditions with murky water before. And making the adjustments, found the fish biting again.

Take everything into consideration when it comes to conditions. For instance, in the summer months you may find television viewership go down drastically. Why? Because more people are outside during the warmer seasons, working in the garden, mowing lawns, camping, vacationing, waterskiing, and yes, fishing. So, changing bait may mean focusing more on marketing with mediums that accentuate warmer weather activities.

Work hard, have fun, and keep casting your line!

THINGS YOU SHOULD NOT DO.

Before I get into all the things you should be doing to better market yourself and your books, I want to take a moment and explain the things you should not be doing. There are some things that may bring you short-term profits but will ultimately lead to long-term problems. Yes, you may make a cheap sale out of the tactic, but you will create a reputation for yourself that will damage your long-term goals.

These tactics are not worth it. Unless, of course, you have no long-term goals, and merely want to sell as many books as you can within a year or so and then move on to something else, it's not worth it. And even with that, why bother with books? I mean we are talking about products with some of the lowest profit margins you can hawk. Why waste your time selling something that will yield so little when you could focus on products that will have a much larger payoff?

But, that's not the case with most authors who are guilty of the things I am about to talk about. Most of these people think this is perfectly acceptable, and that he or she must do anything possible to sell as many books as possible (no matter how) in order to continue moving up the ladder.

The problem is when you get a reputation like this; no one wants to associate with you. Because they do not have to read the tea leaves to predict the outcome…and no one wants to be associated with the outcome.

And let's face it, most of these are douchebag tactics.

So, the following are just a few obnoxious selling tactics you should avoid:

• Don't trick someone into purchasing your book. Don't show your book to a friend or family member (or someone who helped you with it!) in a private conversation and then say, "I hope you like it. The book is $15.95, but most people just give me $20 because I donate the difference to the Humane Society."

• Don't turn every conversation into something about your book or books, trying to make a sell. Let's say you are having a conversation about a popular movie. "The main character is not as believable as the protagonist in my latest book. I happen to have a copy right here." Or politics. "It reminds me of the political unrest in my latest book. I happen to have a copy right here." Normal conversation should never be nothing more than a transition onto a sales pitch.

• When at a convention, do not walk up and down the isles and corridors, asking passersby to pose for a photograph with your book...and then say, "That's $10.00, would you like me to sign it to you?"

• When participating on a panel at a convention, don't hog up all the time talking about your books, not allowing the others on the panel to fully participate. The other writers and the audience members will make fun of you (naming you) to others behind your back for the rest of the convention. Trust me, it happens.

• Don't send private messages on social media sites (especially to people you do not know) with the sole intent of pushing your books. You look like an idiot. Also, do not send a friend request with the same intentions.

• Never post something to someone else's timeline or site that does nothing more than promote your work... especially without permission! I had one person send a friend request on Facebook. Within seconds of my approval, he posted a short story of his to my timeline, asking my friends to read and check him out. I ripped the story to shreds in the comments. Publicly. It was a ferocious critique. He deleted it himself. Never had that problem since.

• Do not make comments on others' posts in social media to promote your work. "I agree! This is why I wrote my latest book..."

• And please do not take the opportunity to promote your work in your birthday wish on social media. "Happy Birthday! You should treat yourself with a copy of my latest book that you can buy using the following link..."

• Or even worse, offer condolences and promote one's work in the same post! "I'm sorry your mother has passed away. Maybe if you read something funny it would take you mind off things. My new book has a lot of funny things you might enjoy..." No, really, this has happened more than a few times!

• Then there are those who manufacture sympathy,

saying he or she is facing some financial distress, or a family member has passed away. And if people would purchase their new book they think it would help them cope with the loss. Again, I have seen this more than a few times!

• I have a friend who said an author once sent her a "special" Yom Kippur message, which had a link to the offender's Christian fiction! My stomach hurt for hours after laughing so hard over that stupidity.

• Don't add anyone to any groups on social media without permission. Especially if it is nothing more than a disguised group to sell your books.

• And *never* post a review for someone else's book (good or bad) and then post a link to your own work.

Hopefully the majority of you are reading these and thinking how horrible these examples are, and that surely no one would ever do such things. Well, that is where you are wrong. Everything mentioned has happened. Either I have witnessed it firsthand, or a friend has seen it and shared the experience.

The goal of this book is not to trick people into purchasing your products. There are some tactics listed that will put you in a better position without coming across as pushy or manipulative, but you never want to be the hardcore salesperson.

Now, here's the thing I want you to think about. How many successful authors do you know that does any of the above things? How many full time writers do these things? How many "big name" authors are guilty? None. Why?

Because those tactics would have prevented them from getting to the place they are now. So, don't be a jackass. Just write the best books you can and promote them within the lines.

FREE MEDIA OUTLETS

Let me start by giving you a little personal background. I started working in retail sales after a brief stint in the United States Marine Corps in the mid-'80s. From there I began a career in broadcast radio as an on-air personality. I learned that talking to an audience on a daily basis was marketing, playing the right music, making sure the commercials had the right message in order for the clients to see enough success to continue purchasing ads.

It didn't take long before I was working as program director and then general manager. At one point I managed eight radio stations simultaneously ... I'd like to point out I had a full head of hair up until that point. But seriously, that's when I became aware of the importance of marketing. Since those beginnings, I have worked as marketing director or chief marketing officer for newspapers, television stations, health care companies, and automotive entities.

So, this book will focus on varying aspects of marketing for writers.

Unfortunately, too many writers today think maintaining a Twitter or Facebook presence is the only marketing plan they need. Now, don't get me wrong, there's nothing bad about social media and its role in marketing, but if you want to go further, you need to do more.

This brings us to the question as to how much

marketing you are willing to do as a writer. Let's be honest, most of the bigger publishing houses are not expecting you to do much. Therefore, you have the luxury of marketing as much or as little as you desire. And if you want to write and not be bothered with marketing, that is up to you. Nowhere in my words will you ever find me saying you have to market to be a writer.

Dealing with the smaller presses, however, will more than likely be a different story. Most small press publishers will expect the writer to market his or her product as much as possible for the project to be worth the effort.

As I mentioned earlier, social media is good, but it should not be your foundation in marketing. It should be an integral part of the overall marketing reach, but never the main focus.

First of all, I want you to think of your writer identity as a company. Now think of everything you do to bring attention to yourself, your books, or your works as streams of revenue. You will see that social media networking is only (or should be) a small portion of the overall revenue coming in for your identity.

I actually created my horror industry writing identity with marketing in mind. I chose a pseudonym (Knost) that alphabetically puts my works and products on bookshelves between those of Stephen King and Dean Koontz.

Since we are thinking of our writing identity as a company, and the marketing things we do as streams of revenue, we want to focus on avenues that will not cost us money. There is no better publicity than free publicity. And that's why press releases and interviews are so important.

Now don't be afraid to think big here. This is where many writers fail ... they all too often think on a smaller scale. I suggest you focus on television, radio, and newspapers.

Look, these media outlets are searching for stories every day. They would love nothing more than to have something fall in their lap.

Do not make phone calls or send E-mails with this. You need to prepare what you want to get across, and with the book you want to promote in hand, visit in person. You will want to speak to the news director, program director, or a reporter or manager. You want to speak to them face-to-face. You want to smile. You want to be kind and thankful for their time and consideration. Then you want to give them your spiel. But, you don't want to take up too much of their time.

Keep in mind, it is far more difficult for them to turn you down face-to-face than it would be over the telephone or via E-mail. In the marketing industry we call it building relationships. You need to cultivate as many as possible ... in person.

The next thing I suggest is to make sure you bring them an actual story. Don't just walk in thinking they will do a story on you or your book because you are an author, or that your book just won the Bram Stoker Award®. Give them a story they can sell to their audience.

For instance, let's say you are a single mother struggling to raise two children. You just wrote a horror book about a single mother struggling to keep her two children safe from whatever monsters you have created. You reveal the parallels and monsters in your own life that show up metaphorically in the novel and use them as strengths to make your real life self stronger -- and for others struggling with the same issues to see that there is hope. See what I mean? You give them a real life story so they can promote your works or products.

After everything is said and done, don't forget

the follow up. Handwrite a thank you note and mail it (I intentionally left the E off the word mail there) to the person or persons who took time to talk with you and/or do a story about you. I'll talk more about the power of thank you notes later.

Don't be afraid to see this through. Remember, the first step to success is to take the first step.

INTERVIEW WITH CHARLAIN HARRIS

I had the honor of interviewing Charlaine Harris, who worried she may not be the best person to speak on the subject of marketing. However, I told her I wanted to hear what various successful authors have to say about marketing, including those who think they are not marketing minded.

Charlaine is the New York Times bestselling author of *The Southern Vampire Mysteries* series about telepathic waitress Sookie Stackhouse, which is the basis for the highly successful *True Blood* on HBO. 2005 marked the debut of Harris's new series *The Harper Connelly Mysteries*, with the release of *Grave Sight*. The series is told by a young woman named Harper Connelly, who after being struck by lightning, is able to locate dead bodies and to see their last moments through the eyes of the deceased.

A true daughter of the South, Charlaine was born in Mississippi and has lived in Tennessee, South Carolina, Arkansas, and Texas. She has one husband, three children, two grandchildren, and four rescue dogs. She leads a busy life.

MICHAEL KNOST: I'm sure your marketing tactics have changed over the years, especially from the very beginnings of your career. When it comes to marketing, what are some of the things you remember to be pivotal in those early years of your success and before your success?

CHARLAINE HARRIS: My first book came out in 1981, when marketing was left to the publisher. I really don't think my publisher did much in the way of marking my debut; maybe they sent out review copies. I did get some good reviews. Of course, this was when dinosaurs ruled the earth.

KNOST: What marketing elements do you think are vital to authors?

HARRIS: Word of mouth is still the most powerful marketing there is. But that happens organically. These days, though my knowledge is limited, I would say that taking advantage of on-line promotions is really important. After all, you don't have to leave home to take advantage of these. Guest blog! Promote your own blog. Establish an author page on Facebook. Make your own website interesting and always have some kind of promotion going on it (that is where I really fall down).

KNOST: How important is networking?

HARRIS: Very important. Not only can you learn from other writers, it's very advantageous to be up on what's happening in the industry. It's so helpful to have friends with whom you have this crazy profession in common. Besides that vital aspect of networking, the more friends you have in the industry, the more opportunities you can learn about how to publicize your work.

KNOST: I'm sure book signings are now quite different than they were when you were beginning. But, I was wondering if you could share a few book signing tips for those struggling to build a name.

HARRIS: The biggest difference is pictures. People never used to do that. Now that everyone has a cell phone, they all want pictures. Other than that, book signings are your big opportunity to establish a one-on-one relationship with readers in less than two minutes, basically. ALWAYS BE POLITE. STAY UNTIL YOU HAVE SIGNED EVERY BOOK, IF YOU POSSIBLY CAN. Be prepared, but not stiff. You will answer the same questions approximately 3,000 times if you're lucky. You cannot appear bored or impatient. Though this may be your weariest moment, it is the first time your reader has met you, and that reader is excited and nervous. Respect that. Never forget to thank the bookstore for hosting you.

KNOST: What book marketing tactic do you believe to be least effective?

HARRIS: Relentless pushing, especially when you're on a panel. Do NOT hog the microphone. Remember, the other writers appearing with you also want a chance to shine. Do not interrupt, and do not come with notes. Panels should be spontaneous, unless it's one focusing on a very specific topic you're supposed to know a lot about — the books of Shirley Jackson, or the uses of the supernatural in movies, for example. If you try to dominate a panel, you may earn a reader or two in the audience, but you will alienate five fellow writers.

KNOST: I want to give you a standing ovation right now. In

what ways have your marketing strategies changed after fame and success?

HARRIS: My publisher now thinks of ways to promote me online, which is delightful. I don't really have a strategy.

KNOST: In your opinion, how important are book readings when it comes to marketing and success?

HARRIS: I really hate to read, but I love personal appearances. I found out my strength is participating in Q&A. Though my reading was mediocre, my answers to questions could be both funny and informative. It was something I didn't suspect or expect when I started out. So if you think your reading skills are not exciting, try to think of something you can do that readers will enjoy.

KNOST: That makes a great segue to my next question. What public speaking tips do you have?

HARRIS: Think a second before you answer an unexpected question. Remember that everything you say may be in front of thousands of other people with the push of a button. Unless you are promoting a book with real-world themes, do not engage in political or religious discussion, which should be simply common sense. (Do not argue about the political system in Spain with a reader, for example, which is something I've actually witnessed.) Be gracious in your mentions of your publisher. Do not tear down other writers, even really terrible writers. We are all making a living. Be sure to recommend other writers you respect, and try to name one book you've read recently that you've really enjoyed.

KNOST: What marketing elements do you still put to use on a regular basis?

HARRIS: I check my public Facebook page (www.facebook. com/CharlaineHarris) and my own website (www. charlaineharris.com) every day and respond to readers directly. I blog on the Femmes Fatales website (www. femmesfatalesauthors.com), and on my own.

KNOST: If you were starting out today, what would you most focus on marketing wise?

HARRIS: I would try to make myself more comfortable with/conversant with online marketing so that I could personally handle it.

THE BOOK SIGNING

When talking about marketing, one must always think about building relationships. No matter what aspect you are looking at, building relationships is crucial in finding success. And that's what makes book signings and events so important to us as writers.

Let me preface what I am about to say by explaining there are two types of book signings. They are completely different events, yet look similar in many ways. To the bookstore/bookseller, the event is to sell books, but the author may see it as something more than that.

The first is the event where a superstar author comes into town promoting his or her latest book -- for instance, Stephen King or Neil Gaiman. These authors are there to sign books for fans showing up to see them. They are the rock stars of the literary world.

Then you have the event where the author is not as well known, but is in town promoting his or her book. These authors are at the event to build a fan base so they can hope to someday become a literary rock star.

Occasionally you will have an author with one foot in each category, but generally speaking you will fit into one or the other. And chances are, you fall into the latter.

However, I think the majority of authors in the latter category go about working the event from the wrong angle.

You see, the author trying to build a fan base is doing so one reader at a time, at least that is the thought. They feel that the book signing will not be successful if they do not sell a particular number of book copies during the few hours they are signing for the event.

Your goal should be a little broader. You should be thinking of working smarter, not harder. Now, do not take what I am saying the wrong way -- it is vital to be personable with each person that comes to your table, building a relationship with them personally, but you have bigger fish there to fry.

If you think of a book signing as a two-hour promotion for you, you are wrong, or at least you do not see the bigger picture. Put your glasses on and look around. Who do you see? Who has more buyer influence than you?

The bookstore staff.

These are the people you do book signings for. These are the folks you want to build the strongest relationships with. These people can make you successful in the twinkle of an eye.

Let's say you have a good signing event one day at your favorite bookstore. Let's say you sold forty books. Not a bad two hours of meeting and greeting the public, right? The store is happy, the customers are happy, you are happy, and of course, the publisher is happy.

However, most authors do not consider past the few hours they spend at the table when it comes to these events. But, honestly, the bigger sales happen within two weeks after your event. Why? Because if you have successfully built the relationships with the store's staff, they are going to push your books like you have never seen.

If your books are about ghosts and someone walks in a few days after your event and asks for a particular book about ghosts, the bookseller will help them, but will also recommend your book. Why? Because we love to talk about the famous person we know. The staff members will tell customers how nice of a person you are and that you actually came to their store for an event -- such a down-to-earth and cool person.

I promise you they will double or triple the sells from your event in the few weeks that follow. Think about it: as a customer, whom are you going to believe more, someone trying to sell you a book with their name on it, or someone who sells all the books in the store?

Customers will think of you as a hardcore salesman when you tell them how great your book is. A staff member, on the other hand, can brag on your products all day long, and that's what the customer wants to hear.

This is why it is important to invite newspaper and television reporters to do a story about the event. It contributes to the ripple effect long after you are gone. I heard an author complaining about how a TV station came to his event, interviewed him, and talked about his book and the event at the particular store. He said it would have been nice if the TV station had interviewed him a week earlier so people would come to the event. What he didn't see was for the following few weeks, the TV interview possibly brought dozens of people in specifically for his book.

This is why it is good to learn a few salesman tricks. You are, after all, selling yourself to the bookstore staff. And successful salespeople have a list of clients with whom they are constantly building relationships.

So, bake cookies to put on your table for customers, but don't forget to bake an extra pan for the staff.

Use index cards or your Smartphone to keep track of special information about the staff members. For instance, names, birthdates, spouse names, and children. If a staff member tells you about their fourth grader playing in the Little League tournaments, jot it down. Then, when you ask about the family and how was little Johnny doing with the tournaments later on, you have golden information.

Send cards or gifts for birthdays and anniversaries.

Take photos every chance you get with staff members and post them (with permission) on your Facebook, Twitter, website, etc.

If a particular staff member reveals she is a fan of F. Paul Wilson (and she loves the Repairman Jack series) and you know you are going to see Paul at an upcoming convention, have him personalize a copy of his latest Repairman Jack novel for that staff member.

Then begin booking to return to the store every month or so in order to keep the relationship healthy and current.

BOOK SIGNING TIPS

In the last chapter I talked about book signings in general terms. I thought it would be nice to give you more detailed tips when doing a book event like this. Ready? Let's do this.

WEAR A NAMETAG

I know it's weird, but people are more likely to buy from a salesperson wearing a nametag than not. In fact, J. Keith Murnighan, a professor at Northwestern University's Kellogg School of Management, who studies social interaction, says wearing a nametag can certainly encourage positive communication. "I see your name and, bingo, away we go!" he says. "It opens the door."

He also says that nametags lead to accountability.

"If you're less anonymous, then you're likely to be more responsible, ethical, moral," he said.

Adam Alter, a professor at NYU's Stern School of Business agrees that broadcasting your name could certainly invite friendliness. "Wearing a nametag might signal that you're open to interacting with other people, which might encourage them to approach you," he says.

"There's a theory known as reciprocal disclosure, which suggests that friendships are built on a foundation of mutual disclosure. When you share a piece of personal information — a name, for example — you signal to other people that you're willing to interact with them. In turn, they might open up to you, share a piece of personal information that further strengthens the relationship, and so on. So yes, wearing a nametag might encourage people to approach you."

Also, studies have shown that wearing the nametag on your right side gets the best results. It is thought that wearing the nametag on the right side gives the person shaking hands or greeting easier eye contact with both person and the badge as a way to help remember the name or other available information.

Be sure to create a professional nametag ... don't just write your name on a sticker and slap it on. It's easy to print something nice and get it laminated cheap. I wear mine, which is laminated with a photo of my latest book, around my neck by a lanyard.

USE THE CUSTOMER'S NAME

Dale Carnegie once said, "A person's name is to him or her the sweetest and most important sound in any language."

Boy, did he nail it.

Just as the power of your name on the nametag is important, so is using a customer's name every chance you get.

Remember the song from Cheers? "Sometimes you wanna go where everybody knows your name."

Several years ago I was working as marketing director for a large hospice organization when I met the governor of our state at a particular event. He and I spoke for roughly ten minutes before he moved on to others in attendance.

Two weeks later I was invited to an event honoring the governor. For whatever reason my wife could not make it, so I went alone. While making his rounds, the governor came up to me and said, "Michael, how are things at Dignity Hospice?" I couldn't stop smiling. We chatted a few minutes longer before he moved on pressing the flesh, but I couldn't help but feel so honored that he'd actually remembered me.

When I got home my wife asked how things went. "Fantastic," I said. "Oh, and the governor came up to me and said, 'Michael, how are things at Dignity Hospice?' I must have made an impression on him a few weeks ago!"

My wife smiled. "He remembered you, did he?" She peeled off the nametag I'd forgotten the event host had put on my jacket. She held up the tag, which included my name and the company I represented. "I'm sure he wasn't referencing this."

Have I mentioned my wife really knows how to keep me grounded?

I do want to point out that you should be careful when using a customer's name. If you use it too much, then you may well appear to be attempting to manipulate them, which is likely to have the reverse effect to that which is desired.

Ever had a telemarketer use your name like it was the hot button for the morphine drip?

"Now, Steve, I want you to think about how you, Steve, could benefit from this. Steve, do you think it would work? If anyone could succeed, Steve, it will be you."

Watch the customer carefully when you use their name: Does it relax them? Do they smile? Or do they look a little irritated or tense. If it is the latter, lay off the name-calling at least for a while.

DO NOT OVER-SELL

The last thing you want to do is come across as some kind of face-to-face telemarketer. You don't want customers rushing past your table, avoiding any eye contact, as if you were one of those fancy cosmetic store clerks trying to spray you with cologne.

No one likes a pushy salesperson. Just be yourself … unless you are a pushy salesperson. At which point, be more laid back. Remember, your real goal is to build readership, not pushing products onto people who will be put off with you, more than likely never read your book, and will most definitely take the long way around your table if they ever see you again.

DO NOT UNDER-SELL

On the other hand, don't just sit at the table, avoiding eye contact with passersby. Smile at every person who walks past you. Say hello or hi. You do not have to be aggressive to be engaging, but you should always broadcast an appearance of friendliness and passive salesmanship.

HAVE A CONVERSATION

Don't feel as though you have to talk solely about your books. In fact, having conversations about other things is a good way to sell more books. Let's say a customer walks by with a shirt with your favorite football team on it. "Let's hope they win today!" That could be a conversation starter. It's a good one because the customer doesn't feel as though you are trying to spray him with cologne and hard sell.

The customer feels comfortable enough to stop at your table and chat. As you continue to talk about how the coach needs to let the quarterback throw more during this game, keep an eye on where the customer's gaze is during the conversation. His or her focus will be on you books. You have given him or her a great opportunity to safely look over what you have.

You can transition the conversation to a particular book they are looking at. "That one is a collection of ghost stories set inside coal mines." It's a natural way to get to present your work to anyone.

PUT THE BOOK IN THE CUSTOMERS HAND

Now that you have the customer at ease, and you are explaining what the book he or she is looking at is about, it's time to pull a subtle stunt. It is a psychological trick, but it works almost every single time. While talking about the book, pick it up and innocently hand it to the customer.

I have never had anyone not accept a book I was

handing to him or her. It's a powerful thing to witness. Now the choice is theirs to buy it or put it back on the table. Over the years I have tracked sales according to number of customers, etc. And I have always found that I close the deal (sell a book) 75% more often when I physically put the book in the customer's hand.

Just remember to be subtle when you do it, and be sure you are speaking when you do it. Maybe even about something on the cover, or contributor's list, a story about the artwork, or anything else to get the book in the customer's hand.

IF THEY DON'T LIKE THE GENRE YOU ARE SELLING, SELL YOURSELF

Let's be honest, not everyone is going to like the genre of books you write. So, don't be dismayed when someone tells you, "This looks great, but I don't care much for scary stuff." Keep talking. Keep selling yourself. Be nice, understanding. But, think of other ways to sell them. "I know what you mean, my wife can't go to sleep at night if she reads something too scary! But, I have found there's always someone in my family (you probably have the same in yours) that will read them … will love them."

You just gave them permission to consider who in their family they could buy the book for. Seriously, you would be surprised at the number of scary books I have sold to people who told me they hated scary books. Sell yourself.

YOU ARE NOT THERE TO BUY BOOKS

During the book signing, you are there to sign books. You are not there to shop for books. You are supposed to be at the table greeting the public, not up shopping for yourself.

Now, don't get me wrong, once the signing is over, shop as long as you want. But your time at the table should be spent at the table.

YOU ARE NOT THERE TO CHAT WITH FRIENDS AND FAMILY

Don't get caught up chatting with friends or family members who happen by. We are talking about individuals who are not going to purchase a book. Do not let them keep your attention away from possible customers.

USE FRIENDS OR FAMILY AS DECOYS

However, if you have friends or family who would be willing to help, you could use them as decoys. What I mean by this is when things are slow you could ask them to stand in front of your table and talk. You see, customers see you are engaged with someone else, they do not feel threatened by a sales pitch ... after all, you are busy talking with other customers, so they can step up behind your friends and look at the books on the table.

You should have a code word for your friends to know so when you say it, they walk away from the table, leaving the real customers still standing there checking out your books. They still feel comfortable because they just witnessed you allowing customers to leave without pressuring them to buy something.

I have had friends come and do this for hours and then go out with me to eat afterwards. It is amazing how effective it can be.

YOU ARE NOT THERE TO TALK SHOP WITH OTHER AUTHORS

If you are doing a signing with multiple authors, keep in mind, you are not there to talk shop and have conversations with the other authors. You are there to sell books. There is nothing wrong with having conversations when no customers are around, but when someone comes to the table the conversation needs to immediately cease so you (as well as the other authors) can focus on the customer.

I suggest you talk the other authors into getting together for something to eat or drink afterwards, as we are reclusive beings ... and getting to speak to others like us is fantastic when it happens.

GOODIES

I may have mentioned this before, but I wanted to reiterate how having a plate of cookies, cupcakes, or candy on your table will attract customers. Yes, some will stop just for a goodie, but the majority will chat about your books, and many will purchase. It's just a good way to sweeten the deal. Sorry, I couldn't resist.

These are but just a few tips. I suggest you ask other authors what tips they may have to offer regarding book signing events. We can always learn from those who do it a lot. In fact, I am going to share more tips from other authors in the next chapter.

TIPS FOR BOOK SIGNING EVENTS

I know the last chapter was on book signings, but I wanted to see what other authors have to say about book signing/events. What follows are those tips:

"With everybody and his/her mother having books out today due to increased self-publishing, book signings no longer hold the intrigue or have the professional esteem they once had. Unless a writer is a very big name with a large following, signings more often than not come across like just another bake sale offering cookies few want to buy. The author sits hopefully with a smile she/he hopes is inviting but not desperate while potential buyers glance over and file past on their way to somewhere else. What to do? There is no magic approach, that's for certain.

"But here are two suggestions. Writers should consider offering 'book talks' where the writer gives a short reading and then talks about the book, the research, and the inspiration in order to draw in listeners and, hopefully, buyers. Or writers could offer 'author talks,' where the writer talks about not only the book that is being promoted, but the broader topic of the business and process itself, and is open to answering questions, including the inevitable 'How do I get published?' and 'How much do you make?' And then, of course, push the book and nab some sales!" **– Elizabeth Massie.**

"1) Bring a story to work on in case no one shows up.

2) Remember, if people do show up, they are there to see you. If folks are even near your table, engage them. Make eye contact. Converse with them. Be in the moment with them. I've seen too many authors sit like bored lumps behind tables, playing on their phones or otherwise looking like they'd rather be anywhere else then act shocked that no one approached them or bought their book." **– Maurice Broaddus.**

"Even if your publisher sets up a signing, talk to the store manager yourself beforehand to iron out details. I did one signing in the evening after the store was closed. They locked the doors and they were only letting in people who came to the door for the signing (thereby excluding any casual shoppers). We didn't get many." **– Tim Lebbon.**

"Be real, be honest, and especially if you're fresh, stand up (if you're able). It's a psychological thing. Don't have the folks looking down on you. Keep them at eye level, on an even playground. You'll move more product and garner more respect. It may seem like a little thing, but trust me, it works." **– Bob Freeman.**

"I've been to book signings for rather famous (or at least I thought they were rather famous) authors where I was the only person who showed, and I've endured that as an author at my own signing. If you end up with one of those events, treat it as if hundreds were there; make sure you thank that lone reader and especially the booksellers, since your future fate at that store is in their hands." **– Lisa Morton.**

"Print business cards or fliers: Have a way for cash strapped readers to find you later. Give customers something with your name and where they can find your books." **– Frank Larnerd.**

"I always do book signings with the same blue pen. That way, if I add a personalised message to a book I've already signed, it'll be in the same colour as my signature." **– John Grisham.**

"Remember that everyone in that bookstore supports your way of life. Thank them, even if not a single copy of your book is sold at the event." **– Douglas Clegg.**

"Don't get depressed if nobody turns up. It's happened to many of us." **– Ramsey Campbell.**

Yes, it can be depressing if nobody shows up, but you can always think about that tip from Ramsey Campbell. Because, this is advice coming from one of the greatest living writers -- and if he has events where nobody shows up, you can pretty much guarantee you will, too. Hey, you're in great company!

This next tip is something I stumbled across on the Internet. It is by an author named Holly Becker. Now, I don't know Holly, nor have I ever read anything by her, so I can't vouch for her writing or professionalism, but I can tell you this next tip was one that really intrigued me.

"Why not bring a book for book buyers to sign? I'd never in my life heard of this idea but I wanted to do it ever since I first imagined signing books. I bought a fantastic softcover notebook I ended up using for this purpose. That way, as I signed a copy of my book for my guest, they would in return sign (and often write sweet thoughts to me) in my guest book on my signing table. I remember that same evening, in my hotel room, sitting in bed on cloud nine as I flipped through each page reading each and every note." **– Holly Becker.**

Some great advice from a variety of writers. Remember, what works for some will not work for others. You need to find what works best for you. Once you find what works for you, hone it. Don't just settle for what you know ... work at taking what works well and improve it, or add to it.

Maybe the best advice I can give you is to have fun. Too often I see authors at book signing events who appear as though they were captured by the store employees and were waiting to die a horrible death. Remember this is your spotlight. You should have as much fun as you can. If customers see you laughing and smiling and having a good time, they will be more attracted to you and your books.

PREPARING FOR A BOOK TOUR OR BOOK LAUNCH PARTY

Preparing for the book launch of my novel *Return of the Mothman* last year, I remembered a nimiety of promotional things to do during the week leading up to the event.

I looked at particular dates for the book tour -- determining the geographic locations -- and began jotting down notes. Consider this your outline. I wrote down a date and location and began listing media outlets under each column. I'm talking about television stations, newspapers, radio stations, etc. Now many of these outlets will cross over into various geographic markets -- for instance, a television station may cover three of the cities you will be touring within weeks.

The thing you should do is determine which city or event would be best served by each station or media outlet that covers multiple locations for each individual event. This will make it easier to spread your coverage around in the best possible balance. The reason you do this is a station will give you good coverage on one event, but will not continue to do so over and over. And because of that, you don't want to blow your marketing cache in one event.

That's why it is best to find the best event for each media outlet and save others for geographical events they are more suited for. This is targeting your marketing plan to get a better tour coverage rather than a single event covered well.

Next, begin contacting the media outlets. Don't forget that doing this in person is best. Don't be afraid of asking for the general manager. Go to the top. You have no idea what kind of power these folks have. They can make one phone call and you are getting star treatment. But you won't get that from a phone call or E-mail. Go see them in person.

Have something for them. You can always follow up with an E-mail with all the information they will need ... it's a good reason to get their E-mail address. But, don't get me wrong -- you must have the information with you when visiting in person. Promise to send them the digital files via E-mail, which include photos and other items they would need.

The general manager may introduce you to a producer, program director, news editor, or on-air personality. Be prepared for them to record an interview with you while you are there; however, most will probably schedule a day and time for you to come back for that. And if you are at a radio station, they will set you up for the day and time to come in for the live morning show to be interviewed. If they do not, ask about it. Don't be afraid to come right out and ask what you would like to see happen.

I suggest you maintain a good calendar. You don't want to double book on the same day/time. You want to make sure if you do, you have plenty of time to get from one media outlet to the next without a hitch.

As far as scheduling, you want to schedule your interviews or articles to air or hit stands as close to a few days before the event date as possible. To be honest, a week or two before the event is far too early, and many times the day of the event is too late. So, if the event is on a Saturday, having your media coverage hit on Thursday or Friday is ideal.

Now, this is important. When going to a radio station for your scheduled interview, you do not want to be on time. You want to be extremely early. If they tell you to be at the station at 7:30 a.m., you want to be there at 7:00 a.m. for a number of reasons. The first reason is traffic or other things can cause you to run late. Second, which is the real reason I go as early as I do, is you get more promotion. As soon as I arrive, I make sure someone knows I am there, and that I am scheduled to be there for an interview at a specific time. The reason I do this is because I know the morning show hosts have a strict schedule they have to keep. I know they won't be able to get me on the air any earlier than the time that is set, but it will ensure they will be talking more about my upcoming interview until they do it. They know I am sitting in the waiting area listening to them and they want me to hear them talking it up before I walk in the studio.

Be sure to thank them for talking it up when you walk in. Let them know they made your day by hearing them promote you while you waited. Feed the egos of the people who are introducing you to their listeners. Because if the radio people like you, the listeners will like you.

This is also the reason I say you should always make the hosts look good during the interview. Always make them look like a genius to their listeners and they will make sure the listeners love you, and encourage them to go meet you at your event. What I mean by that is never correct a host if he or she says something that is not true. Make him or her look good.

If a host says, "Nosferatu is the first vampire," you can say, "You are absolutely correct, Nosferatu was the first film adaptation of Bram Stoker's book *Dracula*." And then you could follow up with something like, "I can't believe you knew that!"

Remember, a successful book tour or launch party will depend on good planning/organizing skills, and a work ethic to follow through.

To give you a good idea of how it can pay off, when I did the book launch party for *Return of the Mothman,* it sold out during the event. That was 105 copies of the novel, plus 35 copies of my other books. And I did not have to pay one cent for any of the promotion.

Good luck, and get promoting!

PERSONAL EVENTS

Most book signings are set up so that the author needs only show up and sign books the bookstore has already purchased from the publisher or distributor. In these cases, the author's goal is to sell as many of the books as possible so the bookstore has to purchase more. Pretty simple, right? Yeah, sure.

However, some bookstores buy the books directly from the author, or set up a consignment deal where they will pay for the books that were sold. And then you have events that the author attends: conventions, workshops, special fairs, etc. Here, the author brings his or her own books and sells them personally.

Most usually in these cases, the author buys the books from the publisher at an author's discount and sells them for profit. This is a great way to pay for your convention trips, by the way. And still make a profit!

Some publishers still pay royalties on the books you purchase (at the discounted price), so you make a little more from that end of the equation, too.

The events where authors take their own books and sell them on their own is what I want to talk about because these are good revenue streams for the author. When I teach workshops or speak at writing conventions, I always have books to sell -- especially *Writers Workshop of Horror* and

Writers Workshop of Science Fiction & Fantasy.

Last year my novel *Return of the Mothman* was published. I set up a table for the Mothman Festival in Point Pleasant, West Virginia, for the weekend and made a killing. The Mothman Museum is there in town, and I sold a ton of books to them as well. I bought the books at the author discount and sold them for profit ... all the while still earning royalties on all those copies.

I also convinced my local cinemas to include *Mothman Prophecies* to their list of older horror movies they show every October. I asked if I could set up a table for the showings of the *Mothman* movie and made a killing from *Return of the Mothman* sales.

My point is there are so many opportunities for a writer to set up a table and sell oodles of books. You should be taking every advantage you can to sell from your own table.

But you have to be prepared for this. It's not just something you can throw together within an hour and expect to work out perfectly. You have to make plans early. You have to be prepared for anything.

The first thing you need to do is make sure you have enough books. One of the best sales maxims is you can't sell it if you don't have it. So, you have to work months ahead to make sure you have ordered the books in time for them to be shipped to you before the events.

Make sure you order wisely. If you know the audience ahead of time, you can stock the right books in time. For instance, when I do writer events I know I am going to sell more of the writing books ... if I am doing the Mothman Festival I know I am going to sell more of the *Mothman* books.

Next, make sure you purchase a ton of "Personally Autographed" stickers to put on the covers of the books.

These little boogers attract attention, and for some reason cause many customers to buy as soon as they see them. But that doesn't mean you should pre-sign all your books. Remember, the personal touch of signing in front of the customer is part of the moment they may be purchasing ... and not just the book.

You want to make sure you have a really good sign at your table. I have talked about this before, and it's a fantastic investment. I bought one that retracts into a metal case, which slides into a canvas bag. It's over six-feet tall and really gets the needed attention.

Get a bank bag or a moneybox. A moneybox would be ideal, but I find them a bit cumbersome for just me. A bank bag is so much easier for me to manage and keep an eye on. Go with your preference, but make sure to have one or the other. Get it early.

The next thing is one that so many writers overlook until it's too late. And that is put some money in your bank bag or moneybox. That's right, what are you going to do when you make that first sale and the customer gives you a fifty for a fifteen dollar purchase? I'll tell you what you're going to do: you're going to panic! This is why you go to the bank days before your event and get as many ones and fives as you can afford. Always get the smallest denominations as you will always need them most.

The next thing is something few writers do, and I can't understand why more do not think of it. I'm talking about having the ability to take credit/debit cards. Today's world finds the majority of people walking around with very little (if any) cash in their pockets, wallets, or hidden areas.

I use a card swiper from PayPal, which is free when you order it. It plugs into my iPhone or iPad, connecting via a free app. I have the books pre-stored in the program so when someone wants to purchase them, I click on the books ... the app tallies up how much the customer owes. I swipe the card, have them sign the screen with their finger, and let them choose if they want their receipt to go to their E-mail or text, or no receipt if they so choose. Done.

I have also tried the Square card reader, but I like PayPal's better. Both readers will take the same (very minimal) percentage of the sale, but when using the Square my money goes into my bank account after a twenty-four hour period. On the other hand, the PayPal reader will have my money in my account instantly. I have a debit card through PayPal, which gives me access to my account just as a credit card or debit card. So, I could swipe a customer's card for a twenty-dollar purchase and literally spend that money within seconds via my PayPal card.

Another feature I like about the PayPal reader is if I forget or misplace the reader, I can take a photo of the card with the iPhone, or physically type in the card number and it works. It takes a little more percentage of your sale, but not much more at all.

Be sure to keep the card reader on the table for customers to see. Many will recognize it as a card reader and will know you are able to take credit cards. Also, having a small sign on the table stating you take credit cards is a smart thing to do, too. PayPal sends a nice laminated sign with their card reader for you to use for this very purpose.

These personal events can be profitable, but I think the biggest advantage of these events, however, is being in front of so many different target demographics. Remember, your goal is not to just make a sale ... your real goal is to make a new customer, a new reader.

INTERVIEW WITH DAN POYNTER

I wanted to interview someone about book signings, autograph parties and book launch events, and tried to think of the best person I could find to talk with on the subject. And then Dan Poynter came to mind.

Dan is the author of 134 books and has been in our industry since 1969. He has sold millions of his books, including several bestsellers, for tens of millions of dollars in sales. Many of his books sell at the rate of 10-20,000 copies per year, every year.

His work for publishing was recognized by the Publishers Marketing Association when they gave him the Benjamin Franklin Award. He was given the Irwin Award for the best electronic promotion campaign by the Book Publicists of Southern California. He is a past vice-president of PMA.

Dan's seminars have been featured on CNN, his books have been pictured in The Wall Street Journal, and his story has been told in U.S. News & World Report. The media comes to him because he is the leading authority on book marketing, promoting and distributing.

Dan was prompted to write The Self-Publishing Manual because so many publishers wanted to know his secret to selling so many books. Dan is one of the publishing industry's most energetic, experienced and respected leaders. He lives in Santa Barbara. For more information, visit:

http://parapub.com/sites/para/information/promote.cfm#doc639 or

http://parapub.com/sites/para/resources/allproducts.cfm

Autograph parties, book signings, or book events are a type of product promotion that producers of other goods or services don't have. Bookstores, large and small, chain and independent, are staging events to attract potential customers into their stores. Authors are the draw. I wanted to find out how one of the industry's best handles these types of events.

Get out your highlighter, because you are getting ready to have a mini workshop of producing and maintaining successful book signing events.

MICHAEL KNOST: You are seemingly the authority when it comes to author events. You have sold millions of copies of your books, and you show no signs of slowing down. Why are these book signings and book parties so powerful?

DAN POYNTER: Authors are celebrities. People think if you wrote a book, you know something. And, you probably do. Non-fiction books are written from the best research you can do, you direct your material toward a certain type of reader, and you color it with your own experiences. Book writing is a journey. Often we do not know where the process will take us. We learn everything there is to know about our subject and, in effect, we are gaining an advanced degree in our area of interest: we do the research and then we do the paper. So, authors are pretty special, often interesting, and do know quite a bit about

their subject area.

However, with so many thousands of books being published every year, getting the right exposure, even for a best-selling author requires a well-planned strategy.

Autograph parties are a good ego trip when successful and can help make your other promotion more effective. Often times the publisher schedules these events for the benefit of the author. If the publisher doesn't, you may want to book your own personal appearances. However, unless the author is well known, the autograph party rarely pays off in massive book sales.

If this is your case, it's best to tie in your autographing with a radio or TV appearance and some local advertising. Send news releases, brochures or press kits along with an autographed copy of your book to the local newspaper, radio, and TV station. Notify these people three to six weeks in advance. Don't overlook interested (subject targeted) clubs and community groups who might have newsletters or make announcements at meetings. Think of a timely hook that relates to your subject and present it to all these groups in a novel way.

KNOST: What can the author expect from the bookstore?

POYNTER: The only reason the bookstore is giving you a venue is because you will attract new customers to the store. Any customers browsing in the store at the time of your event are only interested in what they came for. Most of them have never heard of you and do not care about your subject at this particular time. The store may publicize your appearance with a sign in the window for a few days and place a notice in their event schedule. So you must understand that the store supplies the roof and the author supplies the audience.

KNOST: What approach should the author take with book signings and book events?

POYNTER: The right way to approach an autograph party or book signing is simple. "Never do an autographing," says Terri Lonier of Portico Press. "Always offer a mini seminar." An autograph party says, "Come and appreciate me (and buy a book)"; a seminar says "Come, and I will give you something free (information)." Always think of the benefit to the potential customer. How can you lure him or her out of the house and down to the bookstore?

Patricia Bragg publishes health and fitness books. To promote her mini seminar at Borders Bookshop in Santa Barbara, she posted flyers in all the local health food stores. Then she made a mailing to her customer list within a 50-mile radius driving distance. The store was packed and she was on for over four hours—until closing time.

These mini seminars may lead to longer ones for other groups at other locations.

"In today's market, a writer often has to wear many hats, not just as a storyteller, but also as a tireless promoter and a good public speaker—in short, an all-round entertainer."
— Kevin J. Anderson in Publishers Weekly.

KNOST: What advice would you offer authors with regard to these events?

POYNTER: Don't just talk about your book. Everyone knows why you are there; people know you want to sell books. But you must be giving; you must show passion for your subject matter and convince them you are delighted to share this information with them. Be friendly and talk one-on-one as much as possible to the people who are there to listen to you. Make them feel good when they buy your book. Present them with a pen or bookmark that has your book title, your name and the ISBN number of the book imprinted on it. These are great giveaways even to those who may not make a purchase at the time of your book signing.

Some authors put on a professional show using PowerPoint. This kind of a presentation further establishes his or her expertise and makes the evening memorable.

"Don't be one of those writers who seems almost embarrassed at their own book signings. Bookstore owners want a dynamic author who will smile at passing customers, make eye contact and draw them toward the book display. The worst thing an author can do is sit and appear disengaged."
— Lila Guzman

You might even purchase stickers to put on your book covers (give some to the booksellers or specialty retail outlets, too). The stickers can say "Autographed Copy," "Local Author" and "Great Gift Idea" and more. You can have labels printed at a local copy shop. Labels also come on 8.5 x 11 sheets.

Come up with an interesting angle on presenting your subject matter. Perhaps you can have someone interview you about your book or come up with some kind of a contest that relates to your material and awards a prize to the winner. For example, if you have written a cookbook and are having a signing, present a "mystery dish" for everyone to taste. The person who comes closest to guessing the ingredients wins.

When you get to the store, proceed to the shelf where your book will be and look for other books very much like yours. Take them back to the presentation/autographing area. When you speak, take time to hold up the other books (puts your book in good company) and praise them. "This is the book that got me started in this business." "This is the book I keep next to my dictionary for constant reference," and so on. Your audience can purchase just your book or they can leave the store with three or four. Each person can spend $20 or $60. Sixty dollars will impress the store a lot more. And that store will want to stock your book.

Then go to the next chain store. Based on your prior performance, they will want you; they may even have heard of you already. After a few stores, the chain will want your book.

KNOST: What items can an author bring to the table that will help draw attention?

POYNTER: Make a large poster of your book cover. Take your book to a service bureau or to a copy shop. They can print an enlargement on coated stock and will laminate it. Whenever you speak, put this poster nearby, it will serve as a continuous communicator to your audience. Our enlargements are 24" tall.

Fiction is different. Creative writers can't always talk about their subject because they are writing entertainment. No matter, the public usually just wants to see and hear the celebrity. So be witty and charming and nice but tie in the book. Develop some stories about why you wrote it or discuss some of the things you learned while researching it. Think of something interesting about the book that will make them want to buy and read it.

Fiction authors often read a section from their book. It is a special occasion when the creator of a work reads it and gives it oral expression. Ask your audience for questions. This may give you the opportunity to inform, entertain, learn what your readers are thinking and discover what's important to them.

KNOST: How does an author get book signings scheduled?

POYNTER: Contacting stores. If you are organizing your own book signings, approach the stores in your area first; start out locally to learn the ropes. Stores love local authors as they know you have friends who will attend. When searching bookstores for autographings, use sites like www.Switchboard.com. Choose a category (Book Store). Type in a City and State. Wade through a few sponsored listings...and then there they are, including phone numbers, addresses, maps, driving instructions, and more details!

You may also visit a Barnes & Noble store and ask for their National Directory of Stores.

And go to www.Yahoo.com, Regional\US States. Choose a city and the Yellow Pages will give you the names, addresses and telephone numbers of bookstores. Get maximum value from your travels by booking as many appearances as possible.

Contact independent, college and chain bookstores and ask if you may set up a table, erect a sign, and provide some refreshments. The bookstore may be reluctant to sponsor such an event unless you are willing to underwrite some of the cost. The expense won't be small because, in addition to the refreshments and sign, you will have to consider a good deal of promotion via E-mail and even space ads. But the store may pay half. Even if they fail to sell a lot of your books, this event will bring new customers into their shop. Once introduced to the bookstore, they are more likely to return in the future.

E-mail announcements of your appearance to every friend, relative, acquaintance, and prospect within driving distance. Make the event seem big and important. Let everyone in town think that everyone else is going, and that if they don't go they will be the only ones not there.

Given a choice, try to schedule the signing for later in the month. Bookstores usually publish their event calendar on the first so an event in the last two weeks will be promoted longer.

Help the store draft the description of your book. Stress the benefits you want people to focus on. Have a 25-word and a 50-word description ready to go.

Suggest that some of your books be placed behind the

sales counter or on the "Staff Recommendation" shelf.

Also ask the store for their media list so that you can contact the editors and broadcasters yourself.

Create a small flyer, well designed, colorful and professional looking of course, to give to people as they enter the bookstore. You might be surprised to see that many will approach your table that might otherwise have never known you were there for a book signing. Get someone else to distribute these flyers; don't do it yourself. Just make sure the person handing out the flyers is friendly and appears to be enjoying meeting people. This is your one chance to make a good first impression.

KNOST: What about tips for book launch parties/readings, etc.?

POYNTER: Place a copy of the book on each chair that is arranged in the signing/discussion area. This will encourage each attendee to hold, look and think about purchasing the book. Often, if you can get your book in a reader's hand, the sale is nearly made.

If the store allows, post laminated articles from your local newspaper or magazines about the book to be featured. This can enhance the value of your book-signing event.

During the signing, don't just sit at the table. Give yourself presence! Make yourself visible! Whenever the opportunity arises, walk around the store with your book in hand and introduce yourself to the customers, especially the ones who are eyeing books in your genre's section.

Bring gifts for the staff such as Tee shirts or a box of chocolates. Make an impression on them. Don't forget to have food on hand. As I mentioned earlier, you will need to discuss this in advance with the store. Cookies, coffee, and fruit help attract potential customers.

Bookstores will sell the books for you. In other venues, the money collecting may be up to you. Have someone in the back of the room handle book sales so you can spend time talking to people.

Bring a guest book for the attendees to sign so you can create a mailing list. Try to get email addresses and phone numbers so the next time you're in that location, you'll have more people to send announcements to.

Bring a camera and take pictures of buyers with you and your book. Get a photo of you and the person who arranged the signing. Suggest the photo would look great on the store bulletin board.

KNOST: What are your thoughts on joint book signings? Or multiple author events?

POYNTER: This can be effective especially if the other writer or writers have written books on similar subjects.

KNOST: Do you leave unsold books (owned by the bookstore) unsigned?

POYNTER: No. Wherever you set up book signings, remember to autograph the store's copies of your book. They are more likely to sell, and bookstores cannot return books to the publisher if they have been autographed.

"Remember, there are lots of stores that don't carry your book. But if you do a signing, they have to carry it."
—*Raleigh Pinskey, 101 Ways to Promote Yourself.*

Always follow up with a nice note thanking the person who arranged the signing. They will remember you.

KNOST: Any tips for scheduling book tours?

POYNTER: Make arrangements to visit friends and relatives in other states. Find out what bookstores are available to you in their respective areas and contact them. Firm up a few book signing dates. Call the local radio and TV stations in advance and request an interview the week of the signing.

Try to coordinate your tour with a relevant marketing period. For example, if you have written about a romantic subject, you could plan your tour during early February, near Valentine's Day. There are times, too when you want to avoid booking a tour, such as during election periods when the media is covering political events. (Unless, of course, you have written a political exposé.) You should also probably avoid touring during major sports events. It is hard to compete with the Super Bowl.

Some days will turn out more people than others. Coordinate your signings and tours with your publisher or distributor. Make sure your books will be in the stores. Call the store to make sure they have books and bring a carton of them just in case.

When traveling, plan longer layovers between flights. Contact the airport bookstores about a signing. Suggest

they order the books from Ingram or your distributor. Stop in and autograph the books. This is not a regular signing (mini seminar), you are just autographing the books. The store will place "autographed" stickers on the books and that will help sell them. Now your books are in that airport store.

KNOST: How does one get booked with the national chain stores?

POYNTER: Contact them.

BARNES & NOBLE.

Book nationally by calling Donna Passanate at the corporate office, Author/promotions dept. at (212) 633-3300.

Barnes & Noble has more than 520 branches. Local store coordinators are called "Community Relations Managers." Call them if you need special equipment such as a projector screen. Calling the local store helps the CRC remember you and may get your book on the Staff Recommendations display. Some may even make up brochures for the checkout stands and send notices of your appearance to local print and broadcast media. See Store Locator at www.bn.com

Here are the Community Relations Managers and their phone numbers for different areas in the country. For the Northeast area, call the corporate office number (212) 633-3300.

Mid-Atlantic: Randy Losapio (212) 750-4093 Midwest: Sarah DiFrancesco (651) 697-6201

Southeast: Anne Lee (407) 898-6993 Southwest: David Hamrick (512) 328-5526

West: Alice Anderson (510) 433-4367

"When it comes to doing a coast-to-coast tour, the best thing to do is to contact our Author Promotion Department and they will help you set up your schedule and make the connections for stores all across the country." -- Marcella Smith, Small Press Business Manager, Barnes & Noble.

BOOKS-A-MILLION

To set up book signings, contact the Director of Marketing, at (205) 942-3737; Fax: (205) 945-1772. See the Store Finder at www.booksamillion.com/ncom/books?id=20 69814819835&stores=1

¾Little Professor Book Centers www.littleprofessor.com

ATLANTIC BOOKS

(610) 629- 6040 www.atlanticbooks.us/index.html

Hastings Books

Michael Knost

(615) 904-9755

CHAPTERS (formerly Classic Bookshops and Coles Book Stores) 468 King Street Wet, Suite 500 Toronto, ON M5V 1L8

Tel: (416) 364-4499 Fax: (416) 364-0355 www. chapters.indigo.ca/

KNOST: What is something that most new writers overlook when it comes to these events?

POYNTER: How to autograph a book. Autographing books is something you will be asked to do both in person and by mail. It is surprising how many prolific authors have never given much thought to how they might autograph a book. Confronted with an admiring fan, they are suddenly at a loss for words. Most authors simply sign: "To Kathy with best wishes," add their signature and sometimes the date. At times you want to be more personal, such as thanking a contributor for his or her help and support on the book. If there is something special about the buyer, include it in your autograph.

Often, there is a time consideration. On a mail order book, you can dream up something special, while at a well-attended autograph party it is difficult to think about a few well-chosen words while trying to give witty answers. And, by the way, especially when rushed, make sure you spell your buyer's name correctly. In all the hustle, it is easy to draw a blank and misspell the simplest name or word, ruining a book and disappointing your fan.

"To autograph your book to a stranger is easy, to autograph for a friend is difficult."
— Rex Alan Smith

KNOST: What other book events tips do you have?

POYNTER: Don't overlook fundraising event autograph parties. Here, you would do the selling and would donate part of your proceeds to the club or organization. An event like this often gets press coverage in the local newspaper. If there is a popular celebrity involved in the cause, all the better for you and your book.

When traveling, drop in on bookstores and when you find your books on display, offer to autograph them. (Remember that autographed copies cannot be returned to the publisher.) An autograph makes the book more valuable and this will provide an opportunity for the staff to become familiar with you and your book. Sometimes you will wind up doing an impromptu presentation.

Book fairs such as Book Expo America, have autographing sessions. You can expect to sign and give away about 300 books in 30 minutes. The fairs set up special autographing stands and you sign up for a half-hour stint.

Some authors autograph a number of books before an event so all they have to do is add the name of the individual. Just be sure to use the same pen color. Don't pre-autograph books in black and then take a blue pen to the event. Not only does it look pre-planned, it disrupts the continuity of the autographed page.

THE RADIO INTERVIEW

I touched on the radio interview earlier, but I thought I would go into a little more detail in this one. I've mentioned my history in broadcast radio a few times, especially when it comes to managing radio stations, programming, marketing, but I started out as an announcer or personality. I anchored a few morning shows and had a blast interviewing many stars.

Now that I am a writer, I get to sit in the opposite chair. I know how it feels on both sides. I know what each side wants and how to give or get it. Because of my experience in this, I've always wanted to write an article about how to give a good interview -- because it seems most writers do not know how to be interviewed.

I know that sounds strange; how hard is it to sit in front of a microphone or on a telephone and answer questions? Well, to be honest, you should be doing more than just answering questions. In fact, you should be doing far more than simply answering questions.

The first thing you need to do is outline your goals for the interview. Make sure you have notes on hand so you do not forget the important things you want to cover or bring out. Not just notes about what you want to talk about, but also what you want to accomplish with this particular interview. That could be as simple as noting that you wish to promote your newest book. It could be to promote an upcoming book signing. It could be promotion for an upcoming event you are participating in, like a book festival, convention, or library event.

It is also very important to write out the station call letters (WKRP), its music format (Rock), the name of the city (Cincinnati), and the names of the hosts. Then use the names as you are talking as you would in normal conversation.

The most important piece of information I can give you is to not make your interview an infomercial. If all you are going to do is sell your product, then you are going to be very boring, maybe even annoying. You have to give the hosts information about you, your life, and things not related to your product. In other words, have a conversation. One of the best interviews I ever had was with "Footloose" singer Kenny Loggins. We talked about his kids and how he handles fatherhood, the things he does to support their daily homework assignments, and his general viewpoint of the public education system. Sure, we talked about his music. Sure, we mentioned his latest release. But, we had a fantastic interview because we had a fantastic conversation.

The next most important thing you need to understand is you are not trying to make yourself look good -- you are trying to make your host look good. I am amazed while listening to writers talking over the hosts, interrupting them, and so forth. I actually heard one tell the host of an internationally syndicated program he was wrong about something menial -- nearly argumentative.

Look, if you make the host look good, they will talk about you for days. They will also push producers into inviting you on the show more often. You make them look good, they, in turn, make you look good. You can disagree with a host, but do it in a way that he or she looks as though they are geniuses. For instance (as I mentioned earlier) if they mention that Nosferatu was the first recorded vampire, instead of calling them out on the falsity, incorporate their answer with the truth -- and begin with the word "yes" or "that's right." For instance, "That's right, Tom, Nosferatu was the first movie based on Bram Stoker's creature." You make the correction ... while making the host look like a genius.

Next thing is to research the Show before the interview: The old saying about knowing your audience is true, but knowing your host is equally important. If your host is a shock jock, be ready for something crazy. And if you're on an FM morning show, expect pop culture. Listen to shows in advance. Hosts are consistent. If he or she debates someone on their show, expect a debate. Not all hosts are nice! Even if you don't live in the host's market, chances are you can stream their show online through their website or apps like TuneIn Radio, I Heart Radio, and Radio.com.

Be prepared to talk about your book as though the host never read it. Because, I hate to tell you the cold hard truth, there is about a 90% chance the host did not even see your book's cover. Some do read it, but most do not. They do read summaries of the books, but they get hundreds of books and speak with authors every day, so they don't have time to read all the books that come their way. Sorry! Try sending them a summary with the key points. This makes the host's job easier, and you're likely to get a better interview.

Which brings me to another great point. Send the hosts sample questions for them to ask. They may never use them, but at least the questions could give them an idea of where to go with their own questions. Make sure you know the answers to the questions you provide. And be prepared for all questions. Especially when they say, "Do you have anything else you'd like to add?" Be prepared to answer it by going back to your notes.

Speaking of notes, do not read from them verbatim. The notes are to remind you of elements, they are not meant to be cheat sheets with exact answers. This will keep you from sounding as though you are reading the answers. And trust me, if the host or the listener thinks you are reading your answers, they will turn you off.

Finally, be yourself and have fun. Don't try to be someone you are not. Because you will come across as something you are not, and that's not always a good thing. Make sure you have a bottle of water and breath mints with you. You'll thank me later for those last two.

SIGNS OF THE TIME

When you are out doing book signings or speaking engagements, how professional do you look? I'm not necessarily referring to your attire or grooming habits, I'm speaking more about the items you have representing you on the table, or around you, other than your books.

If you want customers, fans, or the general public to perceive you as a professional, then you must make every effort to make the best impression you can every time you attend an event.

Keep in mind, perception is reality in the mind of the customer, fan, or browsing passer-by. So if you're sitting there with homemade business cards that look as though they were printed on a dying dot matrix printer, or signs, posters, or bookmarks that look cheap and cheesy, guess what the perception of you will be?

Seriously, it doesn't cost very much at all to pay for quality business cards. We're talking about cards that will look professional. The same goes for bookmarks or posters or flyers, etc.

You should seriously consider hiring a graphic arts professional to design your items. If the items look amateurish, guess who is perceived as the amateur author trying to hawk his or her wares? The more professional your promotional materials look, the more professional you will be perceived.

I have been fortunate to have great cover karma, which means the book covers of my books have been really nice -- So it is easy to get signs with the book covers on them to make me look better. I have used foam backing on large signs that looked great but these were not the easiest to transport.

Not long ago I found a fantastic way to have my cake and eat it, too. And you know I love eating cake. I discovered a sign system with a six-foot by three-foot vinyl sign that retracts into a metal enclosure on the floor. Retracted and put away, this beauty is roughly the size of a large roll of wallpaper -- and it comes with a canvas bag for easier transportation. The neat thing about this system is you can replace the vinyl (with a new image) anytime you want, as you have the hardware that will last for several years.

I recently purchased one of these systems and have the *Return of the Mothman* artwork on it, along with information about yours truly and the new book. I am amazed at the copies I am selling with the sign behind me as opposed to the number of books I sold on average before displaying the sign. It is unbelievable. I have people asking if they can have photographs taken with the sign.

Now let's go back to attire and grooming. What should you wear while doing public appearances? Honestly, that is up to you and the type of books you will have on your table ... and the type of event you are working. You don't want to look sloppy or unkempt -- and you certainly want to look clean.

But the most important aspect is you want to look approachable. You want to be as inviting as possible. Always keep that in mind when it comes to your attire and jewelry and piercings, etc. Never allow your style or persona to stand in the way of meeting new fans.

This is important because I see authors who have a certain persona that makes them a brooding individual who often puts on a costume of shock, just for the attention. Look, I have nothing wrong with how anyone dresses, but if you are hoping to reach as many people as possible, you should take an honest inventory of how you come across publicly with what you put on your body.

Now, if your hair is dyed red, purple, and black, you have body piercings, nose rings, tattoos growing on your body like kudzu, and you are wearing all black leather, then you are going to come across as an imposing figure. Please, don't take me wrong, I'm not saying to not allow your appearance to go into these realms, I am merely stating you should take a personal inventory and honestly ask yourself if you appear open or inviting to the majority of people frequenting the events you are involved in.

The biggest problem with the person with the above appearance is he or she usually does not make an effort to speak to anyone. Again, the persona is quiet, mysterious, elusive, eccentric, brooding, etc. This is what I want you to get: No matter how you appear physically, you should always do everything you can to be inviting, friendly, and charming. That can be done with even the weirdest appearances.

If you have an iPad or laptop, why not create a high quality PowerPoint presentation to loop on your table? Again, professionally done, these not only make you look professional, but they can also capture the attention of folks walking by. Keep your looping presentation short, sweet, slow, and at the highest quality possible. Utilize your book covers in these as much as possible, and photos of you and fans, etc.

Which brings me to my final point. Be sure to take a camera with you or a smartphone with a camera. Ask fans or buyers if you could take a photo with them for your Facebook page or Twitter or Web site. Make sure the camera is a good one and you always make the fan/buyer look great.

Now, include these photos in the PowerPoint presentation for future events. Not to mention, you have invited someone to friend you on Facebook because they want to see the photo ... and you didn't even have to ask them to friend you.

I love getting the fans/buyers involved, so any way you can make them feel special, do it. As I mentioned earlier, maybe you could put a journal book on your table and after you have signed a book for someone, ask them to sign your journal for today's event. Ask them to write whatever they want. You will be surprised at how fast you will grow a following this way.

SELLING BOOKS IN UNUSUAL PLACES

When it comes to marketing books these days, bookstore appearances are simply not enough. If you want your books or your name brand to have a prosperous life, then you have to start thinking outside the coffin.

In the old days the traditional bookstore book signing event was paramount to every author's marketing plan -- it was practically the only avenue you could take. Over the years, however, authors have found it is increasingly difficult to secure book signing events in bookstores. Authors not only clamor to get space for their books on the bookshelf, but jockey for space on the bookstore's floor for book signings.

However, if you start making an effort to match venues with your book topic, you could very well attract success with book signing events. You can increase book sale profits by appearing in unusual places.

The first thing you need to do is identify viable venues for your particular book or books. Topic + audience + opportunity = sales. What's your book about? Who are your readers? Where do your reading audience members hang out? Answer these questions and you'll soon develop a list of potential places for book signings.

For example, if you write a book about computer

troubleshooting, what better place to set up a signing than in a computer store on a busy weekend afternoon? Have you written a children's book with puppies or kittens in the story? Target pet food and supply stores as potential partners for hosting a book signing. If you're a romance novelist, Victoria's Secret comes to mind. And your autographed book of poetry will make a great Mother's Day gift ... from a Hallmark store event.

But you have to approach these venues with book signing benefits in hand.

What you gain from a book signing is obvious: book sales. Yet, to attract the interest of a potential venue, you need to focus on what that venue will gain from your book signing. For example, the store will receive free publicity from any of your marketing efforts, including media, and, of course, a percentage of the sales made that day. The longer your list of benefits is for the store, the greater your chances of striking a book signing agreement.

You may have great success with small and independent stores and businesses simply because you will likely be dealing directly with the owner or manager and can avoid the red tape associated with franchises and corporations. Yet don't dismiss approaching large businesses and stores. Many have the authority to approve a handful of events each year to provide community support, eliminating the need to get corporate approval.

The next thing you want to do is get books into the store.

The inventory process for small stores is fairly easy since you are dealing directly with the owner or manager responsible for inventory acquisition. Corporate and franchise businesses have a much more complicated approval process for adding your book to inventory.

However, you may be able to work out a simple, temporary consignment arrangement. The store buys a certain amount of books to cover the book signing and can return the rest for a full refund. Be sure to suggest the store keeps a small inventory of signed books for people who may miss the actual book signing schedule but come to the store looking for the book. If consignment sales go well, your book may automatically be added to inventory.

You will then need to put together a simple, low-cost (but highly effective) marketing plan.

Marketing your book signing is not expensive or difficult—it simply takes a little preplanning. Print up inexpensive flyers or bookmarks for the venue to use as bag stuffers a few weeks prior to the book signing. Be sure to discuss this idea with the venue ahead of time to make sure there is agreement to use them. Invite the venue to send out an announcement about the book signing to its customer mailing or E-mailing list and put a notice on its (and your) Web site about the upcoming event. You can also hand out bookmarks during the event to buyers and non-buyers alike -- make sure the venue's name and your Web site are both included on the bookmark.

Remember to market your event to the media. Local media are happy to promote local authors and your unusual location for the book signing will be of specific interest (another benefit to mention to the venue). Contact media well in advance of the event AND on the day of the event.

Once the event is over, be sure to express your appreciation to the store for hosting your book signing. Follow up with a handwritten thank you note. The impression you leave with the venue will be remembered when you're ready to promote your next book!

It comes down to the classic sales mantra you've

heard me mention more than a few times so far: building relationships.

Once you start nurturing these relationships you will find that the benefits of your caring for both sides of the deal will mean more benefits to your side. No matter what you do, make sure you make the venue look good. Make sure they are portrayed in a good light. Make sure they truly are benefiting from the event ... don't just selfishly strive to sell books.

You can also do the same for local events, conventions, festivals, etc.

Pharmacies are one of the best types of venues for me. I know that sounds odd, but if you find drug stores that sell a variety of merchandise, they are perfect for books. I sometimes sell more books at a pharmacy event than I do at a traditional bookstore event.

I work with a pharmacy that sells a great deal of seasonal merchandise. This particular company also has a flower shop inside with balloons, cards, etc. They create personalized baskets as well -- I'm talking about baskets filled with candy, snacks, coffee mugs, and anything else that would fit the customer's need. They always put my books in those baskets. It's an automatic sell every time. And it's all because of the relationship I have built with them.

Free your mind from the normal avenues and, remember, there's plenty of fruit along freshly blazed trails.

THINKING BIG

So often we hear or read the cliché *Think Outside the Box*. That's not bad advice, but let's not forget the great ideas that are still inside the box -- the tried and true things that have worked over the years, and continue to work. I like to think inside *and* outside the box.

But when it comes to marketing, you should focus on things with which you are comfortable doing. However, you should never disregard anything you perceive as uncomfortable without at least giving them serious consideration. You never know, you may realize it's something doable.

For instance, let's say you've been invited to be a guest on a radio station to talk about your latest book. You are terrified at the thought of speaking live on the air. Try to think of solutions that would make you more comfortable with doing it. You may not eliminate the terror, but you might be able to make the experience less frightening. Maybe you have a friend or someone who can go on with you -- maybe that person is another writer or someone who's read your book and has knowledge of its subject matter. Maybe your book is a medical thriller and you have a doctor friend who maybe helped you with keeping the facts straight. Whoever it is, you must feel comfortable with them conversationally.

Just remember, if it is another writer, remind him this

is about you and your book. You don't want him to start talking about his works, etc. You can help him get scheduled for his own interview. A good friend will be there for *you*.

Don't be afraid to think big. Then don't be afraid to act on it.

My novel *Return of the Mothman* came out last year. The Mothman creature is a huge phenomenon in my home state of West Virginia, so I've been thinking of ways I can do things no one else does.

I contacted my local cinema complex and spoke with the owner. She knows me, knows I am a writer, and is a very open-minded person. I told her that, if possible, I would love to see if she would be interested in bringing the original movie of the Mothman (*Mothman Prophesies*) from 2002, which starred Richard Gere, and was based on the 1975 book by the late John Keel.

I told her she could purchase copies of *Return of the Mothman* from the publisher at a retailer discount and offer it in the ticket price for the showings. I promised to come and sign/personally inscribe every copy during both showings.

She loved the idea and she decided to set up a table for me and allow me to sell my books before, during, and after each showing of the movie. She refused to take a cut of the profits, and helped promote the event during the previews of movies in the weeks prior to the event.

It was a huge event and I sold hundreds of books.

Now this event may not have happened. The owner could have turned me down. However, the point I'm trying to make is: it would never have happened had I not thought big ... or was too afraid to act on those thoughts.

Thinking big does not mean thinking outside the box. Thinking big just means you are thinking on a grander scale ... a bigger event ... something you would at first think you do not garner such star power to adequately pull off. Thinking big allows you to fill the box. In other words, it takes away the fears of "I'm not big enough to do this," and frees your mind to explore every crevice inside that box before you venture outside it.

Yes, doing a book event in conjunction with an older movie could be considered thinking outside the box, but the scale of the event is what I am hoping you grasp. Think of the box as a TARDIS -- it's bigger on the inside. Don't be afraid to aim high. Don't be afraid to shoot for the top. Don't be afraid to go big. If it doesn't work, you can always scale it back.

I have folks always asking me how I landed some of the biggest names in the industry to participate in my anthologies and writing books. I give them the same answer: "I just wasn't afraid to ask them." I wasn't afraid to think big. If you're an anthologist, why would you not want the best stories from the biggest names? You will never get them if you do not ask.

Thinking big doesn't always mean an enormous scale, either. Imagine you have a book signing scheduled next week. That's certainly inside the box, right? And it's not a monstrous event, is it? Yet, if you think big, you may have a few things you can do to give the impression of a bigger event.

For instance, professional signs give the perception of a bigger production. Balloons and cookies on your table do the same. Maybe you can persuade several of your friends to attend and stand near your table to chat ... then you all go out together that night for a drink or dinner. The perception of those people standing near your table gives an impression of a bigger event.

And by the way, I discovered this next bit by accident.

I have found that when two or three people are standing in front of the table talking to the writer, customers are more likely to stop to see what is going on. They feel safe looking over the shoulders of people at the table because there is a *comfort* cushion between them and the person they are afraid will try to hit them with a hard sell. And you should never hit anyone with a hard sell. People hate it.

But, there's nothing wrong with luring them in with candy. Did that sound creepy? I hope so.

Remember, think inside the box -- think outside the box -- just don't forget to think big.

MARKETING FOR THE SOCIALLY-CHALLENGED

Marketing seems to come easy to many of us. Those of us who are extroverts bask in attention. We have no problem talking with hundreds of passersby during a book signing. We jump at the opportunity to promote our books, websites, and ourselves on a television or radio program. And we are definitely in our element while reading excerpts from our latest works in front of crowds of any size.

However, there are many authors who are terrified at the thought of having to do anything remotely close to the above scenarios.

You may be one of these authors. Don't feel bad, you're not alone--in fact, a friend of mine, a well-known writer in our circles, asked if I would address the subject in this column because she's a hopeless (her word) introvert trying to bring more attention to her work rather than herself.

The first thing I would suggest is for you to not be pressured into doing anything you are uncomfortable with. And that includes pressure you bring on yourself in order to keep up with the literary Joneses of the world.

Never do more than what you are comfortable with. Now, don't get me wrong, we all have discomfort occasionally--I mean, I still get nervous about doing certain events, and I push through it. However, there are certain things I would not be comfortable with doing. I would not be comfortable stripping off all my clothes and donning a sandwich board promoting my newest book. Okay, maybe I would, but I am an extrovert.

But seriously, don't force it. Don't try to pretend you're an extrovert. Let's be honest here -- the majority of readers will probably relate with you far easier than with a loud-mouthed socialvore, feeding off the attention of others, like myself. You will connect at a much deeper level when being yourself -- even admitting your fears of public appearances and starting conversations with strangers.

Most of the time, at least in my experiences, I have found introverts to be great conversationalists. They may not be comfortable with speaking to a group of people, but they almost always do very well when it comes to one on one. Why is that? Because introverts are great listeners. Those of us who love to hear the sound of our voices would benefit greatly if we would follow suit in that regard.

Introverts are conversationalists because they are more than happy to allow the other person to speak as much as he or she wants. And because of that, the conversation is just that: a conversation. That means two people are sharing thoughts and ideas ... it's not a salesperson dominating the exchange. It's real.

So you should consider how many strengths you have by being introverted. People who are extroverted tend to be bigger risk-takers. Introverts, on the other hand, don't feel the urge to constantly take bets and try new things. Being calm and unmoved in the face of opportunity is an asset. An introverted approach is an asset when it comes to selling a product (your book). Being pushy and demanding, as extroverts often are, usually make people balk at the thought of dealing with them. You know what I'm saying; you avoid the carnival barkers as much as possible. The calm approach that the introvert uses can actually make people feel more confident about an exchange.

Don't be afraid to bring your posse. Having a person or two with you at events can be very comforting. Maybe this person is your spouse, or best friend, or even another writer. If their very presence puts you at ease, then make sure you bring them along to get you through the long run.

Your friend can also interact in conversations with you and potential book buyers, taking the heat off you to perform alone. And remember, these friends or colleagues do not have to be extroverts--they can be just as introverted as you are, but together you are both able to speak a little more boldly to potential readers.

If you are at a book signing or a public event, prepare a few conversation starters that you feel comfortable with. Maybe you mention what your book is about, maybe you comment about something the potential reader is wearing, or maybe you introduce yourself as a helpless introvert, asking them to be patient.

Having conversation starters prepared can take the hardest part of conversation out of the equation. It's difficult to be the first to speak. It's difficult enough to have a conversation with a complete stranger as it is! However, if you have a set of starters at your disposal, you will find it easier to get through the tough parts and move forward. Guess what? Most of us extroverts do the same thing.

And finally, I would suggest you embrace the anonymity of the Internet to network further than you would be comfortable to do face-to-face. Facebook, Twitter, and whatever will be the hottest online networking site next week are all great ways for you to speak in small doses when you are ready. You are not put on the spot for an answer while someone is staring at you. You can think before you answer. You can make sure you don't say stupid things. You are able to walk away, then come back and finish.

The most important thing is to find the things that work for you and do them. Don't just use your shyness as an excuse to not do any marketing. Find the things you can do and be consistent in doing them. Take baby steps and keep moving forward. Keep in mind, your marketing strategy should be the same as your writing philosophy: If it doesn't move the story forward, it should probably be eliminated. If you have things you do in marketing your books that do not move your strategy forward, then you may be wasting your time. Just as making sure you are using the right words are important in the craft, making sure you are using the right marketing strategies are equally important.

INTERVIEW WITH DIANA GABALDON

Diana Gabaldon is the author of the award-winning, #1 New York Times bestselling Outlander novels. You can find her on the Internet at www.dianagabaldon.com or Facebook: www.facebook.com/AuthorDianaGabaldon or Twitter: twitter.com/writer_DG/

MICHAEL KNOST: Over the years you have built a tremendous readership base. Other than great writing and fantastic storytelling, what do you most attribute that to?

DIANA GABALDON: Word of mouth. As my beloved first editor used to say to me, "These have to be word-of-mouth books, because they're too weird to describe to anybody!" This is true. It isn't possible to describe what I write in twenty-five words or less, and the traditional "elevator pitch" simply doesn't work. What does work is for someone to rush up to a friend, grab them by the metaphorical lapels and say, "You have to read this book so I can talk to you about it!"

Soon after the end of World War II, an ex-British combat nurse named Claire Beauchamp Randall goes on a second honeymoon with her husband to Scotland. They've been separated by the way for six years, and are rebuilding their relationship, trying to start a family, trying to re-discover themselves and each other. One afternoon, she goes walking by herself, and finds a small circle of standing stones. She walks through these stones, and...

KNOST: What tips can you offer to create and grow a solid readership base?

GABALDON: Free samples and public discussion. Given the oddness of what I write and the sheer impossibility of describing it adequately, the only way I've found of "selling" it to someone is to dangle bits of the story under their noses, and lure them in. Doing this in a place where people are likely not only to see the free samples, but to have other like-minded people (i.e., people who like books) to talk to about the material generates the word-of-mouth I mentioned above.

...disappears, into 1743. Where the first person she meets is a man in an 18th-century army officer's uniform, who looks just like her husband—and in fact, turns out to be her husband's six-times great-grandfather. Unfortunately, he also turns out to be a sadistic bisexual pervert, and...

KNOST: Do you think marketing for a book series is harder or easier, and why?

GABALDON: Easier, because of the word-of-mouth aspect. The essence of the sort of books I write is a constant desire on the part of the reader to know "And then what happened?" Having a readership of any size that wants to know the answer to that question provides you with a lot of free exposure, because they all discuss what might happen next, talk over what has happened so far, argue among themselves, ask you questions—and in general, keep the pot boiling for you, as long as you give them small bits of fresh fuel from time to time.

In a series, too, people are inclined to become very invested in one or more of the central characters—something that doesn't happen if you change characters with every book.

...while trying to escape from the wicked Captain Randall (known as "Black Jack Randall"), she falls into the hands of a gang of roving Highlanders, who are also trying to get away from Black Jack, for other reasons. Bemused by finding an Englishwoman in a place where no Englishwoman should be, let alone one in what appears to them to be her underwear...

KNOST: How has the television series changed your marketing strategies?

GABALDON: Really, not at all. I do what I've always done—but that said, the television people do a heck of a lot of their own marketing, all of which both increases the visibility of my books and (a not inconsiderable advantage) provides me with a whole new range of content to employ in my usual venues. I.e., I now have access to a huge quantity of photos of attractive actors, video interviews, other people's entertaining blogs about the show, and tons of fan-art, which I can use in addition to my own material (which consists not only of snippets of the actual books/novellas/etc., but my commentary on various things).

...they scoop her up and take her back to their castle,

with the intent of finding out just who—and what—she is. Captain Randall would also like to know who and what she is, and demands that the Scots hand her over. Knowing full well what sort of man he is, the Highlanders are reluctant to do this, and so...

KNOST: How does mega-fame help and/or hurt your personal marketing efforts?

GABALDON: See above. The more readers/viewers you have, the greater the word-of-mouth effect—and having a huge corporation that can afford to plaster the name of your work all over tall buildings and buses certainly doesn't hurt.

...they force her to marry one of the young clansmen, so that they can claim she's now a Scottish citizen, and can't be compelled by an officer of His Majesty's army. So Claire is trying to escape from the Highlanders, get away from the castle, and find her way across an unknown countryside in a land where she doesn't speak the language, to the circle of standing stones and her beloved husband. At the same time, though...

KNOST: Do you think keeping in contact with your fans is important?

GABALDON: Pretty vital, I think.

...she is falling in love with the young man she's been obliged to marry. And all the time, the wicked Captain Randall is hunting them both...

KNOST: How do you best do that?

GABALDON: Mostly online venues: I began (in 1985) with the Compuserve Literary Forum, and as the internet evolved, I adopted/adapted whichever services seemed most useful to me. Right now, I mostly use Facebook and Twitter, with a personal website that serves mostly as archive and noticeboard of upcoming events, but which I use intermittently as a blog (sharing material from the Facebook page, for the most part. I'm a big believer in recycling material, so will post a #DailyLines piece (a 2-300 word snip of something I'm presently writing) to Facebook, to my website, and to Twitter (via TwitLonger). If I remember, I'll post it to Goodreads as well, but I use that site much less often because there are limitations on the interface that make it less useful to me).

I do also do personal appearances, but while that's a very popular thing to do for the fans, it's less and less important in terms of overall marketing—and you have to balance the attraction of personal interaction (which is not inconsiderable) against the loss of time (also not inconsiderable. It's great to go and talk to the fans and sign their books, but a four-hour event will cost me two days of work, given the exigencies of travel).

KNOST: What strategies have worked for you when it comes to book signing events?

GABALDON: Back in the day, when there were still mall bookstores, I'd do signings there, sitting at a card table with a small pile of books. People would wander by and occasionally stop, pick up a book, and ask, "So...what kind of book is this?" (The publisher, out of desperation at being unable to describe it, had gone to great trouble to design a lavish, attractive cover—but one that carefully didn't indicate much, if anything, as to the book's content.)

For a while, I'd reply on the basis of whom I was talking to: if it was a young woman, I'd say, "Oh, historical romance, men in kilts, you know..." If it was a young man, I'd say, "Oh, fantasy. Time-travel, magic stones, swords. You know..." If it was a slightly older lady, I'd say, "Oh, historical fiction. If you liked SHO-GUN, you'll love this!" A slightly older man, "Oh, it's science-fiction. I've been asked to write up the Gabaldon Theory of Time Travel for the Journal of Transfigural Mathematics in Berlin, you know..." (That's actually true.) And if it was a much older gentleman, I'd say, "Oh, it's military history!"

This worked fine. All those descriptions are completely true, and all those different people bought—and apparently enjoyed—the book(s). But after a bit, I began to attract larger crowds, with a mix of genders and ages. So at that point, I switched my strategy. When someone asked what sort of book it was, I'd say, "I tell you what. Pick it up, open it anywhere and read three pages. If you can put it down again, I'll pay you a dollar." I've never lost any money on that bet...but I've sold a lot of books.

KNOST: What marketing elements (that work well for you) do you think most authors overlook?

GABALDON: Frequent free samples. Most authors don't post any of their actual work, or if they do, it's a single excerpt that stays up for months. Mind you, most authors don't write the sort of thing I do—enormous books, written out of sequence, and easy to pick brief,

entertaining chunks out of.

Oh, what's that you say? You want to know what happens next...?

KNOST: Knowing what you know now, what marketing aspects would you focus on heavily if you were starting out in the business today?

GABALDON: The same ones I now use: online exposure of my work and my personality, personal interaction with fans, occasional personal appearances.

KNOST: What precautions do you take to protect your name brand?

GABALDON: I don't take any. What I write is so idiosyncratic and identifiable that the chances of anyone a) stealing the bits I post and b) being able to do anything with them, is virtually nil.

How important are book signing events and personal appearances?

At a certain point in an author's career, they're valuable. And a bit further on in said career, the publisher wants you to do them because—while they likely don't increase overall sales of a book noticeably—personal appearances during the first two weeks of a new book's release do have the effect of loading more of those sales into that time period, and that will drive a book that's already likely to be a bestseller higher up Da List (the New York Times list, that is).

And if your marketing depends heavily on the attraction of your own personality and the image of your accessibility, then personal appearances increase that factor.

KNOST: What marketing mistakes have you made that you learned from?

GABALDON: Really, I can't think of any. As noted, my marketing strategy is pretty simple; publishers and TV producers have their own (assorted and various) marketing ploys, which all help my books, directly or indirectly, but as for direct marketing on my part, I'm essentially just doing what I've done from the beginning—just magnified by the effects of expanding social media—and it seems to still work.

MARKETING FOR HALLOWEEN

I don't remember how old I was, but I do know I was very young. It was getting close to Halloween, and my mother and father were working hard on my costume. I wanted to be an astronaut, so they worked at piecing together what looked very much like a spacesuit. It was fantastic. Every detail was perfect and looked authentic -- including the space helmet.

We had an old space-age television set that didn't work. It was white and perfectly round, and hung from the ceiling by chains. It was a little bigger than a basketball, and had a plastic screen that looked just like an astronaut's face shield. Dad gutted all the electronics from the set and cut a hole in the bottom so it would fit over my head -- it looked exactly like an astronaut's space helmet.

On Halloween night my next-door neighbor's father took his children and me trick-or-treating in the wealthy neighborhood. We absolutely racked up on candy and goodies. I had a shopping bag practically full, and was still ringing doorbells when we reached the house that turned everything upside down.

As my chubby little finger moved closer to the doorbell, the front door opened quickly and noisily. Jumping nearly out of my skin, I noticed an old witch standing at the door and cackling eerily. We were all so terrified that we slowly began backing up to get off the porch, when all of a sudden another witch came running from around the side of the house, screaming wildly and heading straight for us!

I turned around so fast my space helmet stayed in place—meaning it was now on backwards and I couldn't see a thing. But that didn't stop me from running! I was screaming with everything in me, and running as fast as my little fat legs would carry me. Candy and goodies were flying everywhere (the neighbor's dad related to my dad later) as I was literally running for my life.

I was heading blindly for a huge tree when my friend's dad finally caught me. Well, I thought one of the witches had grabbed me so I kicked and fought like a wild man. Mr. Shepherd could barely hold me because he was winded from running after me, but probably more so because he was laughing so hard at the whole situation.

As horror writers, we are coming into the best time of year to sell our books. And we should be having as much fun as those two women dressed as witches, terrorizing the trick-or-treaters!

It seems everyone gets in the mood to read something spooky this time of year even if they do not normally read scary stuff. This is why it is important to understand you don't always have a "target demographic" when it comes to readers.

They may be seasonal shoppers of the macabre, but their money is just as green as the money in your wallet or mine.

So, how about some marketing tips for the Halloween season?

First, I would suggest you take advantage of the occasion at your signing table.

Spend a few dollars to decorate a little. Maybe you

could get a Halloween-themed table cover, a costume to wear for the event, or put out a nice bowl of candy.

When it comes to the candy, you want to use it as conversation starters. So, you hold the bowl up for a potential customer and say, "Trick or treat?" If they say treat, give them a piece of candy and work your book into the conversation. If they say trick, have some cheesy gimmick of a trick where you pretend to chop a (fake) finger and give it to them. Then, go into your same spiel about your book.

This is also the season to speak at your local libraries, schools, or community groups. Everyone is looking for someone to speak on spooky subjects. It's not hard to book yourself for the whole month of October weekends this way.

Make sure that when you give your talk, your book or work is included. You should bill yourself as an authority on the subject. Give a true presentation ... not just fluff and a huge sales pitch -- do a real presentation on whatever spooky subject you want. Do the research. Make it interesting. Make it fun. Basically you are selling yourself. If they buy you, they will buy your products without you asking them to do so.

Also, talk with the library or whatever organization is sponsoring the event about putting together a costume contest for attendees. Make sure to include prizes for various age groups, etc.

And do not underestimate book readings!

Which brings me to something I am planning this year.

I am putting together a team of folks to help me with this to make it memorable. I have a number of friends who are fantastic singers and musicians, and I am volunteering them for a few awesome nights.

I am going to create Halloween carolers. That's right,

you heard me correctly ... Halloween carolers.

I'm arranging a number of songs for us to perform door-to-door in select neighborhoods just as Christmas carolers would do only the night before Halloween. The Addams Family theme song, The Monster Mash, and a few others will be the songs we perform. Then I will have the singers hum something soft and spooky while I read excerpts from my new book Return of the Mothman.

We'll have flyers printed up with information about the book -- and where to get it -- to leave with each family, along with Halloween candy and goodies.

We plan to have everyone dressed up in costumes and carrying miniature jack-o-lanterns. We have men, women, and children planning to take part, and they are more excited than yours truly.

And since this is the season for scary stuff, television stations, radio stations, newspapers, etc., are actually searching for things to cover related to Halloween. This is your time to shine!

But remember, give them a reason to interview you. Make some community event be the focus because the media needs to fill time with community events. They need you more than you need them. You just need to figure out how you can wrap an entire community event around you and your books.

Another thing is don't be afraid to approach organizers of local haunted houses or ghost walk trails. You could partner with them and set up a book table before or after folks go through the scary experience. Put up a sign that says, "I am selling nightmares." You would be surprised at how many people will purchase a horror book at an event like this.

Bars are another great place to do spooky readings

and signings. Most of the time, patrons are laid back, de-stressing, and having fun with friends. And bar owners love anything new they can offer their clientele.

No matter what you plan to do, just remember to have fun. Halloween is a time for children ... no matter how old we get.

This year, step out of your comfort zone and do something for Halloween you have never tried before. Even if it is something as simple as dressing up in a costume, or approaching a television station about your holiday ideas, just do something different.

SERVING THE SERVERS

It doesn't matter if you are selling car stereos, beauty products, radio airtime, or books, chances are much of the marketing tactics are going to be the same. So, it's always good to find the things successful marketers do to sell more.

I started selling advertising in my early twenties and have sold electronics, insurance, automobiles, healthcare services and equipment, and just about everything in between.

One of the things I learned early on was being organized is essential. Now, don't get me wrong, I'm not talking about graphing sales reports or studying sales data and cross referencing them from the past five years. I'm talking about taking good notes.

For instance, when I meet a new person who sets up bookstore signings, or is the actual buyer, I make sure to pay close attention to everything he or she says. I focus on them. Then I take notes. No, really, I take actual notes. I write down whatever personal information I learn and file it away.

Now, before I go any further, I want you to know I do not make the notes while the person is speaking. In fact, I wait until I am away from the person before I jot down what I learned. After all, I don't want them to know I am stalking them!

This is personal information I can use in future conversations. If they are married, I get the name of their spouse. I get the date they were married. How long they have been married. Then a few days before their anniversary, I send a personalized card to both names, wishing them a wonderful day.

I do the same with birthdays. And I include little things I learn about them in the cards to make it as personal as possible.

If they have children, I want to know the names and what the little ones are into. If a certain child is playing soccer, the next time I see the person I ask how Johnny is doing in soccer ... or did they win the game last Saturday?

Now, keep in mind, this is nothing more than notes for you. However you want to do it is up to you. Some folks use index cards, putting all the notes on the card and referring to them just before walking into the store, etc. But, to be honest, with today's technology, it is easy to make notes and files on a smartphone, tablet, laptop, or voice recorder.

When you are genuinely interested in the people in your notes, it will come across that way. Don't just try to use the information for your benefit in order to sell more products. Remember, the first key to good marketing is in building relationships. And you are not taking notes to take advantage of relationships; you are taking notes to do a better job at serving the people who help you succeed.

Think about it, you know so much about your friends. You know what music they like, authors they read, food they hate. You become a better friend by catering to their personal likes and dislikes. This is the purpose of taking notes with your marketing relationships.

Not long ago one of my friends at a local bookstore revealed she was a huge Harry Connick, Jr. fan. I mean a hardcore fan. Well, I learned Mr. Connick was coming to town for a concert and decided to call a friend who is a radio advertising salesman. He was able to get complimentary tickets and backstage passes. Do I need to tell you how much my friend cried when I gave her the tickets and passes?

Maybe one of your friends tells you his favorite fast-food item is the McRib sandwich from McDonald's -- a sandwich that is not on the menu very often. Then you hear the restaurant is selling McRibs for the next few weeks. Do you think your friend would love you for picking one up before making your way into the bookstore for your book signing? You would be a hero.

Now, how does this help your sales? That's easy. When you serve those who serve your customers, you win. If you become friends with the people who influence book purchases with individuals every day, you win.

One friend told me someone came in looking for a particular ghost book and she told the customer if they liked ghost stories they should seriously read *Legends of the Mountain State*, an anthology I edited with thirteen stories of ghosts and legends from the Mountain State. The customer bought it. Yep, that was the same friend I hooked up with Harry Connick tickets and passes.

Now, if you are not around the individuals very often, one thing you should do is remember their names. There is such power in using someone's name. And they love hearing you say it. Why? Because you took the time to remember them. You took the time to recognize them as someone more than just a sales clerk.

I've covered this before regarding book signings, but it's worth stressing again. When you build relationships with store clerks and buyers, they will sell far more of your books after you are gone than you will ever do in the few hours you are at the table. So, make sure you take the time to make those people feel special.

I noticed one friend's new hairdo and she lit up with the most gorgeous smile. She told me her boyfriend did not notice her new hairstyle and was sad. But when I mentioned it she hugged me and was nearly in tears.

The whole point of this is to pay attention to those who pay attention to you. Take care of those who take care of you. If you can remember without taking notes, more power to you. But if you're an old fart like yours truly, you better take notes about every little detail.

Motivational speaker Anthony Robbins once said, "The quality of your life is the quality of your relationships."

I would add: The quality of your success is a result of the quality of your relationships.

MONETIZING YOUR WEB PRESENCE

So, you finally have a nice Web presence with links where visitors can purchase your books. Great! If not, don't worry, you don't have to spend a lot of money to have something look fantastic. In fact, I have mine through Wix.com. Now, this is not a commercial for the web-hosting company, but I can't help but sing their praises. They do a great job, the site looks clean with quality, and it's easy to manage. Check out mine and see what you think: www.michaelknost.com.

I like Wix because I can develop a mobile site at the same time I put together the regular website. And that matters because when someone goes to your site via a smartphone, they want to easily navigate through your pages.

I choose to use the free version, which requires a small Wix logo to appear at the bottom. More power to 'em! However, you could upgrade to get more for your site and no advertising links, etc. if you so choose.

Now, I do pay for my Web URL. I do so because it's easier for folks to remember to type in michaelknost.com than to type all kinds of other words and characters.

But I'm not here to talk to you about site designs or web hosting companies. I want to talk about how you should be making money from the content on your sites.

Yes, you will make royalties from your publisher from your books that sell on Amazon, but did you know that you could also make money from the same Amazon books?

I'm talking about monetizing your sites. I say sites because you may have a number of sites, blogs, social media accounts, etc. And you have a way of monetizing what you promote.

You should first look into the Amazon Affiliate's Program. It doesn't take long at all to get set up and ready to go. There are no costs required for becoming an affiliate member, and you don't have a lot of responsibility either.

Basically, you (the affiliate) create links (via the Amazon Affiliate Program site) that lead to your books on Amazon. com. When someone visits your site, clicks on one of those links, and purchases a book, Amazon pays you (the affiliate) a commission!

But that's not all. When someone clicks on one of your links, his or her computer gets a cookie that lasts for 24 hours, thereby giving you a commission for whatever the person buys from Amazon in those 24 hours. Let's say I click on your link to buy your latest book and then find a life-sized Doctor Who Tardis for $8000 ... you're going to get some sweet Time Lord cash because of it!

And the cool thing is you do not have to fulfill any order. You do not have to pack or ship anything ... just sit back and dream of buying your own Tardis from the extra money coming in.

Now, settle down. You're not going to be retiring because of what you make, but extra money is extra money, right? Just because you offered a specific link rather than another one going to the same product.

You can do the same with YouTube and other sites. Maybe you create video reviews, interviews, or a video blog of some sort. Well, in your YouTube account you can choose to monetize your videos. That means you get paid a percentage of advertising that comes on during your video.

And let's not forget that you have the ability to sell products on your site as well. Maybe you have the ability to purchase your books at an author's discount. Then you could create specific package deals customers could only get from your site. For instance, I have two writing books I've published through two different publishers. I can purchase the books and sell them together at a discount the buyer could not get anywhere else. And I can personally sign them.

And don't just get your brain locked onto products. You can promote services such as manuscript critiquing, editing, writing workshops, online writing classes. No limit to what you can offer. Now, now, keep your mind out of the gutter. Although a link to Craigslist could do that for you as well.

Also something to consider is Pay Per Click (PPC) advertising networks. Google AdSense is the most popular option under this category, but there are also others. Basically you need to sign up with the network and paste some code snippets on your website. The network will then serve contextual ads (either text or images) relevant to your website, and you will earn a certain amount of money for every click.

The profitability of PPC advertising depends on the general traffic levels of the Web site and, most importantly, on the click-through rate (CTR) and cost per click (CPC). The CTR depends on the design of the Web site. Ads placed above the fold or blended with content, for instance, tend to get higher CTRs. The CPC, on the other hand, depends on the niche of the website.

Mortgages, financial products, and college education are examples of profitable niches (clicks worth a couple of dollars are not rare), while tech-related topics tend to receive a smaller CPC (sometimes as low as a couple of cents per click).

The source of the traffic can also affect the overall CTR rate. Organic traffic (those coming from search engines) tends to perform well because these visitors were already looking for something, and they tend to click on ads more often. Social media traffic, on the other hand, presents terribly low CTRs because these visitors are tech-savvy and they just ignore ads.

And then there are CPM advertising networks. CPM advertising networks behave pretty much as PPC networks, except that you get paid according to the number of impressions (i.e., page views) that the ads displayed on your site will generate. CPM stands for Cost per Mille, and it refers to the cost for 1,000 impressions.

A blog that generates 100,000 page views monthly displaying an advertising banner with a $1 CPM, therefore, will earn $100 monthly.

CPM rates vary with the network, the position of the ad, and the format. The better the network, the higher the CPM rate (because they have access to more advertisers). The closer you put the ad to the top of the page, the higher the CPM. The bigger the format (in terms of pixels), the higher the CPM.

You can get as low as $0.10 and as high as $10 per 1000 impressions (more in some special cases). CPM advertising tends to work well on Web sites with a high page views per visitor ratio (e.g., online forums, magazines, and so on).

I know, much of it sounds like a foreign language to our ears, but if you take the time to read up on them it could be time well spent. Or maybe you have a tech-savvy person in your life that can help you navigate all the navigations!

The thing to remember, though, is there are many ways to monetize your Web presence, and many of them mean very little action on your part.

MARKET SEGMENTATION

Here, put this helmet on. It's not really a helmet; it's an impact suppression device. Why am I instructing you to wear this? Because I am about to engage in hyper marketing speak right now, and I don't want your brain to explode all over this book's pages. So, please, put this on.

I am going to explain this to you in generic terms. I have worked in this my whole adult life and can get lost in this stuff, so I must apologize now for giving you an ice cream brain freeze without giving you ice cream. Seriously, put the helmet on.

I think we can all agree that it is impossible to be all things to all people, therefore, it's wise to target specific segments of your market, particularly if you are in a smaller business. Not only will this allow you to reach more of the people who will ultimately buy your product, but targeting segments may also reduce the competition you face. (And as a side note, your competition is not other authors.) Finding your niche is often the key to success for small and medium and even larger businesses.

Your market may naturally be segmented by price, quality, region, customer age, income, buying behavior, industry, or anything else. Typically, price and quality are the most evident, followed by product use and the benefits consumers get from using the product. Some segments will be very distinct, and some will be more subtle.

The best example of market segmenting is illustrated in the automotive industry. Yes. they're all cars, but they come in all levels of luxury and utility, price and quality, etc. Some may even cross over into more than one segment, or move from one to the next.

Determine the segments of your market and describe the ones you are going to target. Keep in mind that your products (you are marketing more than books) might cross into several market segments. Finally, remember to address each of these segments when you are planning your marketing activities.

Target Audience

Determining the right target audience is probably the most important part of your marketing efforts, because it doesn't matter what you're saying if you're not saying it to the right people.

You could be the finest computer salesperson alive, but if you are focusing all your time and money on targeting members of the Amish community for a new model laptop, you're wasting far more than time and budget.

Dig into as much detail as possible about who your market is. Describe your typical customer in detail. What is the age group, gender, education level, family size, income level, and geographic location. For business-to-business markets, make sure you include the industry type, company size, job titles/departments, annual revenue, and geographic areas. Have a general picture of who your market is, and then back up that information with concrete numbers and statistics about the size of your market.

Determining the size of your market really requires that you already have a good profile of your typical customer. Once you know "whom" you're looking for, you need to take into consideration things like the aging of the population, and regional variations in income levels and education levels.

Your product offering will also require that you consider not only income levels, but also disposable and discretionary income levels. The former refers to income after taxes that is used to pay for daily living expenses, and the latter refers to income that is left over after those necessities are paid for and can be earmarked for luxuries.

Getting to this level of demographic data will probably require market research. Look for data about the regions where higher densities of these specific groups can be found. The Bureau of Labor Statistics and the U.S. Census Bureau have information about annual spending levels in the major categories of expenditures. You can also find data about age group concentrations in specific regions.

Psychographic

Even though you may have determined your demographic group, people within that group still have very different perceptions about the benefits or value of your product and will be motivated for different reasons. These differences are known as psychographics. To further target your efforts, you've got to determine not only who buys (or will buy) your product, but what makes them want to buy it.

Include as much psychographic information as you can dig up, such as what their spending patterns are, whether they are brand conscious when it comes to your product type, what influences their buying behavior, what promotional efforts they respond to most often, etc. You also want to know how they go about buying it and what you can do to encourage them to buy more. You need this information so you can, in effect, clone your best customers. It is important to really pick apart what motivates them to buy.

The information you glean from a journey into your target audience's brain is often key to your marketing efforts, particularly the positioning of your product. It includes the audience's activities, interests, and opinions. You have to work through behavioral factors, economic factors, and even interpersonal factors to get to the root of purchasing behavior. Answer these questions in your overview:

- What do they like about your product?

- What do they like about your competitor's product?

- What made them decide to buy your product?

- Did they know which brand they were buying before they purchased it?

- What advertising messages had they seen prior to buying?

- How much disposable or discretionary income is available for this type of purchase?

- What are their hobbies?

- What emotional aspects impact their purchase?

- What is their social class or status?

- Who is the actual decision-maker for this type of

purchase?

• What values and attitudes play a part in this type of purchase?

• Who do they look to when making purchasing decisions?

Now that you know your target market and market segments, define your market using concrete numbers and percentages. In other words, how many users do you currently have and how many potential users exist for your product or service? If you are offering a regional service and have found that there are 80,000 potential customers in your geographic area, then this is where you put that information.

One of the biggest reasons all this is so important is the ability to successfully target non-readers. I know that sounds ridiculous, but with the right demo, the right psychographic, and the right message, you can sell books to people who never read books. One way of doing this is targeting the gift market. Anytime someone tells me they do not like scary stuff, I work the conversation to find out if there is someone in that person's life that does like scary stuff.

But, sometimes you have to take Kenny Rogers's advice from the Gambler and know when to fold 'em -- after all, someone from the Amish community will probably never purchase a laptop computer for someone in their family.

THE MARKETING CONQUISTADOR

What are you handing out when you meet people at book signings, conventions, libraries? Nothing? You are missing out on a great opportunity -- or possibly many great opportunities.

You should have two things at the very least: business cards and bookmarkers.

Business cards are perfect to hand out to agents, publishers, editors, other authors, and artists at conventions -- not to mention, media news personnel who are interested in interviewing you. It's professional to have something for them they can refer to later.

You could have two different cards made up if you like. One set of cards would include your phone number and other information you only want specific people to see ... the other set would include a publicly known E-mail address and website URL.

However, instead of two different business cards, I like to give out business cards to professionals and bookmarkers to fans.

The business cards should have all information for those important people to be able to contact you by telephone, E-mail, snail mail, and other available avenues. These would be perfect when you are at a convention and meet an agent who asks for your contact info. You don't look like a jackass by handing them your hand-written information on a stained cocktail napkin.

The bookmarkers should (at the very least) include a public E-mail address, if you promote one, and your website URL. This is a great business card alternative for people you want to look you up on the Internet and buy books, but you do not want them to have your cell phone number and home mailing address.

Bookmarkers are fantastic to have on hand for signings, readings, and personal events as well. One of the sneaky things I like to do is exclude my E-mail address on the bookmarker. I omit the addy for two reasons. First, I make sure my Web site URL is on the bookmarker, which includes a contact page with my E-mail address. This means the person will go to my website and see other things (books, news, etc.) before contacting me.

Second, I like to write my E-mail address on the back of the bookmarker while talking to the fan. I make a big deal out of it ... as though I don't give the address to just anyone. This gives them a feeling of being on the inside. They feel as though they are getting a private E-mail address, and they feel special because of this.

Conquest marketing is becoming a popular trend these days -- especially in the automotive industry. It simply means you are marketing to customers who buy what you sell from someone else. In other words, if you are a Chevrolet dealer, you are trying to market to people who typically purchase Chevrolet vehicles from another Chevy dealer -- hence the conquest aspect.

So, if you think of this in terms of books, conquest marketing is simple, and not as cutthroat as it is in the automotive industry. If Stephen King fans are the perfect target demographic for your book, then marketing to them is considered conquest marketing ... only you don't have to worry about Mister King losing a sale as it pertains to the automotive world. They will still buy his next book, and the book after that, etc.

I mention conquest marketing here because it's another perfect use for bookmarkers. Take a handful of bookmarkers with you every time you visit a bookstore. Find popular books/authors/genres you think are similar to your book or books and slip the markers in the middle of each competitive product. Think about it: You are directly marketing to the exact target demographic with this tactic.

Another way to use conquest marketing is by getting blurbs from popular writers who produce similar works. I can't tell you how many books I have bought by writers I have never heard of simply because a popular writer I loved was on the cover, talking about how much he or she loved the book. That doesn't always mean I will like the new book or author, but it does mean it will get my attention because of the association.

Or maybe we can take this a step further. Let's say you wrote a zombie novel that brings something new to the table ... and that this book also has similar tones to a Joe Ledger novel. Imagine getting Jonathan Maberry to write the foreword. Having his name and his approval for your book is going to be huge for his fans, and those who respect his name and work. Now, this is a step higher because not only do you have a popular professional vouching for the work, but you also have his name directly tied to your product with online searches.

Here's how it works. A fan decides to search Jonathan's name on Amazon to see if he or she has missed any books by their favorite author. Because Jonathan is listed as writing the foreword, your book will show up in that search. That's conquest marketing at its very best.

Now, please do not harass Jonathan about writing a foreword because I said to do it! He's a very busy man with so much on his plate he doesn't have time to look up most of the time. I merely used him as an example because I like promoting my friends in every way I can. Make sure you know someone pretty well before you ask them to do something like that. Don't just use them for your own personal gain. Forge friendships first, for friendship purposes, then, and only then, start asking favors.

The biggest thing I want to stress is this: never take part in conquest marketing in this industry if it is intended to take readers away from someone. The goal is to find faithful readers of works similar to yours and share those readers with the other authors. You are not trying to take them away; you are merely trying to offer works similar to those the readers already love. With this in mind, don't ever try to discredit an author or work because you want the reader all to yourself -- it will backfire horribly every single time.

INTERVIEW WITH KEVIN J. ANDERSON

Kevin J. Anderson is the author of more than 125 books, 51 of which have appeared on national or international bestseller lists; he has over 23 million copies in print in thirty languages. He has won or been nominated for the Nebula Award, Bram Stoker Award®, the SFX Reader's Choice Award, and New York Times Notable Book.

He has written numerous Star Wars projects, including the *Jedi Academy* trilogy, *Darksaber*, the *Young Jedi Knights* series (with his wife Rebecca), and *Tales of the Jedi* comics from Dark Horse. He wrote three X-Files novels, including the #1 bestseller *Ground Zero*, and he also collaborated with Dean Koontz on the novel *Frankenstein: Prodigal Son*, which sold a million copies in the first year of its release. He has written Superman and Batman novels, as well as comics for DC, Marvel, Boom!, IDW, Wildstorm, Topps, and Dark Horse.

He has coauthored fifteen books in the DUNE saga with Brian Herbert, as well as their original *Hellhole* trilogy. His epic SF series, *The Saga of Seven Suns*, is a 7-volume opus that topped international bestseller lists; he is currently at work on a sequel trilogy, *The Saga of Shadows*.

Kevin has a physics/astronomy degree from the University of Wisconsin, Madison and worked for thirteen years as a technical writer for the Lawrence Livermore National Laboratory before becoming a full-time novelist. He is a Board member of the Challenger Centers for Space Science Education and the Lifeboat Foundation.

MICHAEL KNOST: I'm sure your marketing tactics have changed over the years, especially from the very beginnings of your career. When it comes to marketing, what are some of the things you remember to be pivotal in those early years of your success and before your success?

KEVIN J. ANDERSON: Most important, you have to remember that marketing and gaining recognition is like Chinese water torture, drip-drip-drip. You keep trying, a little bit at a time, for years. Each thing you do, each book signing, each keynote speech, each workshop, each panel, might get you one or two new fans. Repeat a thousand times over the years, and it becomes effective. Don't expect to do one thing and suddenly become a superstar.

KNOST: What marketing elements do you think are vital to authors?

ANDERSON: You can't just write good books and expect to be noticed. You also have to be a marketer and a performer. Just like in the record business, you can't just do a studio album and expect to crash the charts. You have to tour, do concert after concert after concert, build a fanbase, expand your social media footprint, and get noticed. A writer can't be a recluse and expect anyone to notice. That might have worked fine for JD Salinger or Harper Lee, but it's just arrogance now. Even major publishers depend on the Author to do the lion's share of the work.

KNOST: How important is face-to-face networking?

ANDERSON: In the past couple of years we have expanded our presence at major pop-culture and comic shows, meeting hundreds (or thousands) of fans every weekend. I find it to be enormously effective—but I already have a large fanbase. I see how it works for our newer authors, though. By personally pitching their books to fans at a show, they can sell more copies of their books in a weekend than normal publishing efforts would achieve in a month or more.

KNOST: What marketing opportunities do you feel authors overlook most?

ANDERSON: Personal talks and selling their own books. Many authors don't want to sully their hands with selling copies, but when you do a library talk (for example) they will often pay an honorarium, and you can get new fans, and you can sell your books. You have to do it all, all the time.

KNOST: I'm sure book signings are now quite different than they were when you were beginning. But, I was wondering if you could share a few book signing tips for those struggling to build a name.

ANDERSON: Chinese water torture again. Drip-drip-drip. Do a lot of signings, local bookstores, local literary festivals, library events, school talks, convention panels. I have driven three hours to get to a signing on a Saturday afternoon, sold 4 paperback books, then drove three hours home...then did the same thing again the following day. After 5-10 years, it has an effect.

KNOST: What book marketing tactic do you believe to be least effective?

ANDERSON: Printing up bookmarks and handing them out. Nobody pays attention.

KNOST: In what ways have your marketing strategies changed after fame and success?

ANDERSON: They get bigger, more ambitious, and I keep building on my fanbase, my mailing list, my social media. I have a good feel for what works and what is a waste of time. I am also less and less patient with "parochial" publicists who try to tell me "You can only promote OUR book and not mention any of your others." That's just stupid, and doesn't do anything to build your audience. I promote all of my books at all of my signings and I try to cross-promote titles with the fans. A Star Wars reader might be enticed to try my Saga of Seven Suns, and a fan of Clockwork Angels might like my Dan Shamble, Zombie PI series.

KNOST: In your opinion, how important are book readings when it comes to marketing and success?

ANDERSON: Book *readings*? Not at all. Very few authors are good readers aloud. Far better to give an interesting and entertaining talk.

KNOST: What public speaking tips do you have?

ANDERSON: Be engaging, find something that the audience is *interested* in. Don't just say "buy my book." That backfires. Give them a reason to want to read your book.

KNOST: What marketing elements do you still put to use on a regular basis?

ANDERSON: Social media, convention appearances, blogs, keynote speeches, giveaways, newsletters to my dedicated mailing list. Building and cultivating my fanbase and caring about them.

KNOST: If you were starting out today, what would you most focus on marketing wise?

ANDERSON: Working with social media and engaging readers, becoming somebody that people will want to follow. That means YOU need to be somebody interesting. You can't just talk about your book all the time, blah blah blah. I spend most of my posts talking about my hikes, favorite microbrews, interesting trips, and I like talking about my work in progress (which is usually a year away from publication, so it's to get readers invested in the project long before it comes out, not just "my book is out, now please buy it!"

KNOST: If there is anything I have not mentioned regarding marketing that you would like to talk about, have at it. I can work up a question for it after wards.

ANDERSON: I can't give away all my secrets! I think this was pretty thorough.

THE MEDIA KIT

The media kit is one of the most important tools for an author or speaker who makes public appearances. It's powerful because it allows others to easily promote you and your books. Not only that, but it's also a good prompt for event coordinators to actually promote outside their building. In fact, I have heard some coordinators say that because I sent them a kit (they rarely see them) they felt obligated to send the materials to their local media outlets -- and ended up with tremendous results.

The first thing I want you to understand is quality is far more important than quantity when producing these kits. So, make sure all the elements in yours are of the highest quality possible.

Before we cover the actual elements to include, I want to let you know you will need a digital copy of the kit posted on your website (or at some web presence) for anyone to download. You will also need to have copies of the kit printed so you can mail to event coordinators, etc. Keep in mind, you should always include a CD, DVD, or thumbdrive loaded with the digital files as well. This will give event coordinators many options with which to work.

The Elements of an Author Media Kit

- An author bio

- An author photo

- Awards

- Reviews

- Blurbs

- Book Info

- Contact details

- Social Media

- Videos

- Sample interview questions

- Bookmarks

- Press release

An author bio

You should consider including two bios: one short, one long. Remember, the more convenience you create, the more likely the event coordinator/interviewer will make use of the material. If you choose to offer just one bio, be sure to make it a long one where the first couple of paragraphs can stand alone.

Think of creating your bio in the same manner journalists create news stories. You want your information structured in the inverted pyramid, where the apex is at the bottom and the base is at the top. That is to say the most important information you hope to get across is in the first sentence. The next most important information is in the second sentence, and then the third, forth, fifth, etc. So if the media outlet decides to cut off the last sentence, you lose nothing.

An author photo

I can't stress enough how important it is to have a professional author photo. This is an area where you need to spend some money. After all, you are building a name brand and your image is built or broken here.

A professional will know how to capture your good side. What I mean by good side is they have the experience to shoot in a way that double chins are not visible, lighting is perfect, and you don't look like a hopeless idiot.

Oh, and don't use cheesy props or gimmicks in the shoot. No skulls or vampire teeth. A professional photographer will try to talk you out of such antics ... listen to him or her.

Once you choose the perfect photo from the shoot, use it for as long as you can. I am talking several years -- especially at the beginning stages of your career, as continuity is a very powerful psychological tool in startups. When you update, keep that one as long as you can as well.

If you can't afford a photo shoot, then find a friend or family member with a great camera -- one who loves photography. Just keep in mind, you need the photos produced in at least 300dpi resolution. This will ensure the highest quality when printed in newspapers and magazines.

And when it comes to the shot you choose, you should produce two variations: one as the publicity still, and the other as the same photo worked into an event poster template. This will include spaces for the coordinators to write in the location, specifics, date, and time of the event. It may be best to go ahead and fill in everything before mailing out ... again, convenience for those promoting the event.

Awards

Listing awards (just as listing good reviews and blurbs) is a very good way to let others brag on you so you don't have to do it yourself. Don't forget to list official nominations.

Reviews

If you have reviews then you need to include a few of the best here. Don't include too many, just keep it short and sweet. Do include the one from the New York Times, don't include the one from your mother as her opinion doesn't carry any weight here (unless she's the editor of the New York Times Book Review).

Blurbs

Blurbs are powerful as they come from your peers, or even

better, your literary heroes. If you write in the horror genre and Stephen King says something nice about you or your book in a blurb, that is a recommendation you can promote with fanfare.

Book Information

Whatever information you wish to impart regarding your book (or books), be sure to give enough details to attract attention and excitement, but not so much that you are over-explaining everything. Just as you want to create story questions in the reader's mind, you want to create questions and interest in possible buyers.

Contact Details

If you've got someone doing publicity for you, or even a publisher, then make sure that their contact details are immediately obvious. If a journalist likes what you have to offer, they will be in touch for a follow up.

If you are a multitasking independent author, then try and provide contact information that looks professional. For example, a phone number and an email address.

Sample Interview Questions

In keeping with the theme here, we're trying to make it easy. Journalists don't want to have to think too much. Give them some sample interview questions that allow you to showcase your amazing personality and your life-changing books. You can be straightforward or creative; it's entirely up to you and depends on your genre. A book on poverty in the third world is going to need a different approach to a quirky Young Adult novel.

You can even list your answers, as it will help the interviewer know where you are going with the answers, giving them insight to follow-up questions.

Social Media.

Provide a list of links to all your social media profiles. People want to see what else you are up to.

Video.

If you have past interviews or podcasts saved, then embed them, or at least provide links to them. Potential interviewers will want to see if you come across well on the screen or if you have an appealing voice.

If you haven't done any interviews yet then I would strongly recommend doing a video interview with a friend, recording it and putting it in.

Bookmarks

This is a great place to include a few personalized bookmarks.

Press release

Include the latest press release for your book. While your press release will of course have been tailored to each and every media contact that you send it to, you should also have a generic one. Put a link to it here.

Okay, so we've got the essentials of your author press kit together. Now what?

• First rule of author media kit success: Keep it updated. New books, new photos, new press releases, new events? Make sure they find their way to your kit.

• Second rule: Make some noise. Generate some publicity. Approach media contacts with carefully designed press releases. You get the idea.

• Third rule: Make it visible on your website. Put a menu item in your navigation bar, right next to the "about" and "books" links.

BEING SOCIABLE ON SOCIAL MEDIA

I want to talk about the importance of social media. Before you stop reading because you think this column will be like all other columns regarding social media marketing, give me a few minutes. I say this because I want to say something different than most others on the subject.

Yes, I do think promoting your work on social media is a good thing, but that's not what I really want to focus on.

First of all, folks who follow you on Twitter or friend you on Facebook because you are an author they love, do so because they are interested in you. You. The person who creates the worlds they love. Please do not ever forget that.

Sure, you can promote your work occasionally, but these people are more interested in you. They love to hear about the movies or television shows you are watching. That means they are interested in the things that interest you.

In other words, they want to see the human behind the monsters.

They want to reply and comment on your posts. This is a way for them to interact. This is a way for them to feel as though they are strangely a part of your life.

When you post something personal, these people care more than most of your own family and non-social-media friends. They think of you as a celebrity, and love to see that you have problems just as they have problems. They love to see the blood under the flesh occasionally...and the heart that pumps it, too.

So, give your followers and friends something to care about.

I have struggled with severe depression for many years. And like most dealing with this horrible thing, I have always tried to hide it. I never talked about it because I was embarrassed about it. After all, telling folks you have a mental illness does not exactly give one the greatest feeling in the world.

However, a couple of years ago I mentioned my depression on Facebook and I received so much feedback from so many wonderful people. I had never received so much support and love in all my life. In fact, I started receiving E-mail and personal messages from people I did not know who are struggling with the same issues. Many of them have told me that because I was so vocal about my problems, and so public with them, they did the same and found a tremendous support group.

They want to know you are real.

Look, for some reason they think we are rich and famous because we are authors. They think we have it made. They think we are eating in five-star restaurants every day, and live in some perfect world. And they love to see when we prove that wrong. They love to see that we are just like them. That we sometimes live paycheck-to-paycheck, and that instead of five-star restaurants, we are more likely to eat at Five-Guys Burgers. They love that we are one of them.

They love when we post things about our family. Now, this is one we have to be very careful with as there are a lot of terrible people out there and you just have to be careful. And you should only do what you feel comfortable with. But, most importantly, use common sense.

With that said, my daughter (seven-year-old) is a huge part of my life, and I include her in my online presence ... with her permission. I never post a photo or video without asking her if she is okay with me doing so. And so far, I have never had a creepy instance to cause me to wish to kill someone ... but we're still early in this game.

Bella and I post videos of us doing science experiments, jokes, etc. We have a lot of fun together and we share just a small part of it with everyone. And I get so many people telling me they love it when we do things together.

On the other hand, I hardly ever include my wife online. It's not because I do not love her, or that I don't want to include her. It's because she is an introvert. That's right, opposites attract, I know. She does not enjoy the limelight. So I leave her out of everything unless she wants in. I love her and respect her more than any person in the world, and I want to protect her from the things she is not comfortable with.

Now, one thing I won't do is political or religious posts. Not because I do not have an opinion on either, but because those posts always seem to get highjacked by people who are so far to one side they can never see anything any other way. And they are there merely to attack and name call ... never to have a sensible discussion. I'm complicated in those departments anyway. I think for myself. I don't follow any group or side, as I agree with a little from each, and disagree quite a bit with all.

So, I don't exactly fit in any neat little box. And better yet, I don't want to fit in any box, thank you ... because those boxes do not define me. And all too often, on social media sites, those boxes do define you because of perception.

What am I saying?

- Don't create your social media sites as nothing but pure marketing databases.

- Bring your personal life into your social media sites.

- But be careful of bringing in too much of your personal life, ideals, or worldview.

And for God's sake, be nice!

Oh, and always use the Type-But-Wait-Fifteen-Minutes method before clicking send when replying to something on social media that pisses you off. Remember, you are more than a person on social media ... you are a brand.

CHOOSING THE PERFECT BLOGGING SHOES

How many miles do you blog a day?

This question reminds me of an encounter I had with a woman several years ago while I was serving as morning show host of a radio station in North Carolina. She heard me speaking to someone at an event and recognized my voice immediately.

"I take you with me on my four-mile jog every morning," she said, smiling.

"You might as well leave me behind," I said with a laugh. "It's not doing me a bit of good!"

Much like jogging, blogging can help maintain your fitness. No, I don't mean health wise, I mean it can improve productivity -- it can also keep your skills sharp.

But blogging for marketing purposes can be dangerous. I mean, think about it. Whose blog would you follow and read every week if all the person talked about was his or her products? Yeah, see what I mean?

This is why your blog should have meaningful content. Now this particularly hits home with me because I am guilty of posting blogs promoting books, upcoming online classes I'm teaching, and availability of writing DVDs, etc.

The best marketing plan sometimes is to make sure your marketing has no marketing in it. What I mean by that is you should (as should I) create a blog to help promote you and your brand without using the content to promote you or your brand.

"Michael! You're talking in circles ... again!"

Sorry. Let's try it this way: when you are posting blogs with real content (stories, opinions, commentary, etc.) rather than blatant promotion (talking about your new book, asking the readers to purchase something of yours), you are building a readership.

As your readership builds, it becomes easier to throw in a promotional post every once in a while without making the reader feel as though he or she is getting a high-stress sales pitch. By doing so, you will potentially reach a larger audience. And hammering promotional blogs every week will atrophy your audience at an accelerated rate.

So, write about things that matter to you. Write about nostalgic things. Write funny anecdotes. Write about horror movies. Write about comic books. Write about the writing craft. You could even write about knitting Cthulhu doggie sweaters.

Whatever interest you have, blog it. Every time you blog you are gaining more readers. And the more readers you gain, the bigger your platform becomes.

I have a few tips that may help you grow your blog:

• Understand your audience. You will have a better idea of what blog content will resonate with them. A good way to test this is to post a quote about something you think you'd like to blog about on your Twitter or Facebook. If you get a lot of feedback one way or another, you know you have something that will get their attention.

• Be honest and open. People love honesty, and it is easy to trust people who are honest. What many bloggers try is just the opposite. They try to showcase themselves as successful bloggers and fake things until they make it. This is totally unnecessary and will only hurt their reputation.

• Be consistent. If you post something only when you feel like it, your inconsistency will stunt your growth. I don't mean for you to be consistent with content or talking about the same thing every time ... I mean consistently put a blog out every week, or every day, or every other Monday, etc.

• Don't alienate your audience with political or religious soapbox posts. I covered this in the social media chapter, but I think it bears repeating here. Unless your blog is specifically political or religious, why take the chance of alienating a percentage of your audience? I mean, why bring your political views into play if your audience was built upon your posts of cooking for diabetics? If politics legitimately come into play in your target subject, you should post a blog that is unbiased in the matter. When you bring your religious views into a blog about the alternative uses for Tupperware, you are not being fair to your audience.

• Allow your audience to participate. Ask for feedback on topics and use what you receive as quotes when you post a follow-up piece. Your audience is made up of people with a plethora of knowledge -- tap into that. Having the knowledge and experience in your posts will not only be beneficial, but the fact that you are also including your community of readers will be incredibly impactful.

• Allow readers to post comments. Great discussions will often ensue after a strong post. And you will find things to cover in future posts by reading and participating in those discussions. You have the ability to maintain decency and order if things get out of hand, as they often do at times. Just keep up the mantra that yours is a community of minds, and that disagreement does not require mean comments or a nasty predisposition.

• Build your platform as that of being an expert on the subjects of which you blog. Remember, you are not just building a platform, you are building credibility. Even if your focus is on zombies, your credibility on the subject may come into play when someone is looking for talking heads on a documentary about the undead. Of course, a documentarian would love to get an expert with a large audience for obvious reasons.

• Have fun. Don't get yourself so wrapped up in the business part of things that you miss out on the fun and excitement when it comes to the subject at hand. Your passion is what brings people to your blog in the first place -- don't lose that with success. Keep going back to why you love it.

The bottom line is if you make your blog about something other than you or your products, you will build an audience that will be interested in you and your products.

THE BLOG TOUR AS AN EFFECTIVE TOOL FOR BUILDING AN AUTHOR'S ONLINE PLATFORM

Something that has become a very popular trend these days is guest blogging. However, truth be told, I am not as familiar with the subject matter as I should be. So I contacted my friend Stephen Zimmer, publisher at Seventh Star Press and fantastic author in his own right, if he would give me some tips to use in this piece. Then, as though a light bulb had come on just over my head, I asked if Stephen would be a guest columnist to talk about guest blogging. Brilliant, I know. Thank you, Stephen for taking the time to do this. Without any further ado, may I introduce to you Stephen Zimmer:

Raising awareness in a publishing climate that sees more new releases occurring than at any other time in history is of the utmost importance to authors of all levels. Effective marketing and publicity in today's indie publishing climate makes use of multiple tools addressing various goals, from sales to furthering the growth of an author's fan base and online platform.

One significant tool in effective marketing and publicity

is the blog tour, as well as related blog site activities. The blog tour is a valuable component of any author's marketing plan for the purpose of platform expansion.

A blog tour involves a number of online activities. These include guest posts, which are essentially online articles on a given topic, interviews, reviews, contests, and creative activities like character posts, which are like guest posts written in the voice of an author's fictional character.

The blog tour involves scheduling either single or multiple activities on set dates at various blog sites. In a way, it can be seen as a digital book tour where the locations are the blog sites themselves. Blog tours can range from just a few days to as long as a month or more, depending on the effort and investment in time and resources that the author wishes to make.

One of the biggest misconceptions among authors out there is that the main goal of a blog tour is to produce instant sales. A blog tour accomplishes very important goals in marketing and publicity, but they should not be looked at as something that generates instantaneous increases in sales. Instead, the blog tour should be seen as an effective tool to build an author's online platform, which sets the stage for stronger sales and more effective outreach in the future.

There are a number of areas where blog tours can be strong and effective.

One of the stronger benefits of a blog tour is their ability to increase legitimate review counts at places such as Amazon.com and Goodreads. The majority of book bloggers are more than willing to cross-post their reviews once they have appeared on their blog sites. This burst in review counts can be very helpful to an author, especially when promotional services like Book Bub often make use of the number of Amazon reviews and the aggregate ratings of a given title as part of the process of determining whether to accept a book for their promotional services.

With a larger and well-respected blog site, blurbs from a good review can also be very valuable for ads, book covers, and other places where a book is being promoted. A review blurb and high rating from a respected review site carries weight with many book readers, and a single blog tour can result in gaining multiple such blurbs in a relatively short amount of time for an author.

Interviews and certain kinds of guest posts can be valuable additions to an author's press kit and Web site, providing more content for readers, fans, publicists, and others interested in learning more about a particular author. In this regard, a blog tour is a great way for an author to produce a nice batch of brand new publicity elements, particularly in the case of maintaining a group of current interviews.

A blog tour can also help increase an author's social media followings, on Twitter, Facebook, and other social platforms, especially through the use of online contests. Contests run through services like Rafflecopter allow extra entries for someone to add an author on Facebook, Twitter, and other social media. If the contest is appealing and the blog site has modest to strong traffic, an author can achieve noticeable increases in followers over the course of a contest. This growth in an author's base can be very helpful in expanding outreach and generating sales in the future.

Blog tours can also be helpful in developing credibility for an author when it comes to the craft of writing or a specific field of expertise. A science fiction author might be a physicist, or a military thriller author a former soldier with combat experience, and a blog tour can help get this known among potential readers.

A good guest post can be seen as an online article, and a post on a writing topic or a special area that the author is knowledgeable about can certainly establish and further an author's reputation among readers. Posts on the craft of writing or about a certain topic which can be useful resources to readers and other writers can bring rewards to an author for a long time to come.

In a nutshell, blog tours and blog activities should be looked at more in terms of growing an author's online platform and media footprint, rather than seeing them as a method to generate immediate sales. In the long run, if an author receives a growing number of good reviews, increased awareness among readers, a growing reputation for their expertise in the craft of writing or about a given subject, sales can certainly follow. But it is important to view a blog tour in the right light, with the proper kinds of expectations, in order to get the most out of them. Blog tours are one of several important tools that should be part of an author's marketing and publicity campaign.

NONTRADITIONAL REVENUE STREAMS

In business, we are always looking for nontraditional revenue, which simply means we are looking at ways at making money outside of our normal product line. For radio stations, it could be something as simple as promoting concerts. It makes perfect sense, since stations specialize in music, and have dedicated audiences.

As an author, you should always be looking for ways to make money that isn't solely focused on typing words into a computer to sell as stories. There are plenty of opportunities to expand. And keep in mind, the best one's will be tied in some small way to you being a writer, or your work as a writer.

Let me give you some examples. I have edited two writing books: *Writers Workshop of Horror* and *Writers Workshop of Science Fiction & Fantasy*, not to mention the book you are holding in your hands right now. Because of the nature of those books, it is easy to see there are many opportunities on the writer side of things. And I mean targeting up-and-coming writers.

For instance, I teach a lot of writing workshops and classes. Conventions, libraries, writing groups, schools, and writing organizations hire me to come and teach various classes on various elements of the craft.

Many of these venues will pay your fee, plus they will reimburse you for all your expenses: travel, food, etc. Of course, while at the workshops, I have a table set up where I sell my books and other products.

I also teach online classes. I have a particular web-based teaching site I use that allows students to see and hear me via video, view PowerPoint presentations, and chat with me and other students during the presentations. I can set my prices and send links to the classes to those who have paid.

I record these classes and burn the files to DVD, which I sell online and at my workshop tables as well. I also produce workshop DVDs specifically for this purpose. I always cross promote my books in the video presentations, which is a good practice with everything you do.

I also offer critique services to writers, where I critique their manuscripts, or edit according to what they need. I work on short stories and novels. In fact, I have helped a number of writers get their manuscript into shape to the point they were published. Now, there are a number of packages involved here because someone may only want a critique, or an overall assessment of the story. I tell them what is wrong with the story and give them tips on improving it.

Another is editing. One package will be extensive to the point that I am pointing out writing problems rather than story problems -- writing mistakes or crutches for the individual writer. And then there are packages for grammar and punctuation, or just plain copyediting. Or maybe someone needs help with a query letter, or a novel synopsis, or something similar.

When I teach live workshops or classes, I make sure I have everything I sell with me at the table. And one of the most important things I have found (that is fairly cheap) is producing brochures. Now, some people print their own from a computer, but I like to have mine professionally printed. They look much better, and the quality speaks volumes to the name brand.

I make sure all my contact information is included, especially personal email address, etc. I want to make sure all students have a way of contacting me, if it is for nothing more than to tell me they just had a story published. The main role of the brochure is to list and explain all the services I do for writers. The brochure breaks down packages and explains what is included in each.

The brochure also has website information, as well as books, prices, etc. This piece is meant to make everything convenient for the possible client. And that is something you need to keep in mind. The more convenient you can make your appeals or offers, the more successful you will be with them. Therefore, the brochure should make everything (including decisions) as simple as possible.

Maybe you are a talented computer programmer, who has created a great piece of software to help writers track their submissions better. Maybe you have created software or a smartphone app that will help edit or format manuscripts. These are things that are considered nontraditional revenue streams.

Tee-shirts with writer content on them, hats, coffee mugs, or even underwear. Or maybe you have characters your fans love -- have a bobble head figure produced, or statues, models of spaceships, games, etc. Or maybe you can write and publish a cookbook with your characters' favorite recipes. We're talking about related products to your book's content.

For instance, if you wrote a book on the best hotdog

restaurants in your state, why not set up book signings at each of the restaurants mentioned in your book? Why not have the restaurants sell your books at their eateries? And why not set up events and book signings where you can take a small grill and sell hotdogs with your book?

I know writers who sell jewelry or hats or monster teeth or steampunk items or flowers or massage lotions or vacation getaways or western wear or stuffed animals. No matter what you write, there are items you could put on your table that would sell like hotcakes because your books are relatable to those products -- it only makes sense because of the books' content.

Whether it is through sales or service, there are many opportunities available for you via the genre or type of books you write. All you need to do is take a good inventory of what you write and what you could do or sell that would compliment each. But, keep in mind, you want it to be natural and not come across as a peddling snake-oil salesman. Keep it relevant and you should have no problems.

INTERVIEW WITH JONATHAN MABERRY

Jonathan Maberry is a New York Times best-selling and multiple Bram Stoker Award®-winning horror and thriller author, editor, comic book writer, magazine feature writer, playwright, content creator and writing teacher/lecturer. He was named one of the Today's Top Ten Horror Writers. His books have been sold to more than two-dozen countries. You can find him online at www.jonathanmaberry.com or Facebook: www.facebook.com/JonathanMaberry or Twitter: twitter.com/jonathanmaberry.

MICHAEL KNOST: Over the years you have built a tremendous readership base. Other than great writing and fantastic storytelling, what do you most attribute that to?

JONATHAN MABERRY: When I was a teenager I was fortunate enough to meet and get to know two great and influential writers -- Ray Bradbury and Richard Matheson. Apart from the advice on craft they gave me, both authors gave me solid advice on how to become a successful published author. They said that although writing is an art -- it's the intimate conversation between author and reader -- publishing is the business of selling copies of art.

Publishers have no obligation to buy anything that they don't feel will sell well. It is in the best interest of a writer who wants commercial as well as artistic success to learn both the craft and the business sides, and to know them well.

A codicil to that is that success can best be achieved by not being a jerk. Words to that effect. Respect, etiquette, fair play, generosity of spirit, a willingness to network and share knowledge, tolerance, and an attitude of positivity are all qualities of successful professional writers. That's the advice I got from Matheson and Bradbury. I've done my best to live by those tenets and, yes, I do believe that this has contributed to my success.

And one other quality helps … flexibility. Matheson also advised to be more than a 'one trick pony'. He said that a writer who wants to make a career out of a business as capricious as publishing should be able to try new things, stretch creatively and adapt to the changing world.

KNOST: What tips can you offer to create and grow a solid readership base?

MABERRY: It's important for a writer in any genre to read the genre -- deeply, too. Know it and be introspective enough to understand what you think and what you feel about it. With that, you should also get to know the readers -- the fans -- of the genre, and you should cultivate a genuine respect for them. They're not just faceless people buying your books. They're people who have dimension and depth and personalities. What draws them to the genre? What draws them to your books? How can you interact with them in ways that are meaningful to

both of you?

When I go on social media, or appear at a conference, or sit down to a signing, I approach this as a chance to participate in a community event. We're all there for a shared reason. Let's have some fun.

Not only does this help me be a happier person, it also cultivates a rich and dedicated fan-base. And I like getting them involved. I have contests to name characters, pick titles, and so on. I make it fun -- and that becomes fun for all of us.

KNOST: Do you think keeping in contact with your fans is important?

MABERRY: I love keeping in contact with my fans. Without them I'm a hobbyist sitting alone in a room. Interaction lets us all share in the fun of the genre. And since I write in several genres, I get to geek out with fans of thrillers, science fiction, urban fantasy, dark fantasy, mystery, young adult, horror, comics ... geez, it goes on and on. I learn a lot from my fans -- about books, pop culture, worldview, and more. And their reciprocal interest helps validate my drive to write.

KNOST: How do you best do that?

MABERRY: One of the things that's helped me grow -- and made it fun -- is social media. I have an assistant who handles some aspects of my career, but I do my own social media. I allot ten minutes out of every writing hour to social media. So if you find me on Twitter, Instagram, Facebook, GoodReads or LinkedIn, that's really me.

It deepens your footprint in the actual interactive fan base, and it allows real-time connection with people who enjoy the same sorts of things I like. We're all book geeks. We're all pop-culture nerds. Social Media allows us to geek out, share thoughts on books, comics, TV, movies. It keeps the water cooler buzz going all day, every day.

It's important to budget your time with social media, though. Otherwise it can absorb an entire writing day. It's equally important to understand it's business potential, and to let that understanding color your online personality. We're writers, so we shouldn't use social media to slam anyone else, we should wax political, we shouldn't get into fights over religion. That's not our brand and it pollutes our message. The tenets of behavior suggested by Bradbury and Matheson can be easily and effectively applied to social media.

KNOST: You've won several awards in the industry; do you think they make a marketing difference? If so, how?

MABERRY: Awards are intended not to praise individuals but to shine a spotlight on the genre or the art form. The Academy Awards, the Emmy's, the Edgars, the Thrillers, and the Stokers -- along with all of the others, draw the ear and tune the ear. They remind us that there are outstanding works being done in a variety of categories, and that maybe we should all lean close and take a look. Or take a bite.

From a personal standpoint, the awards are confidence builders, they drive sales, they've opened doors for me. My publishers have made sure to mention them on the covers of my books. My publishers also mention when their sales teams go to bookstore buyers to pitch their catalog of upcoming titles. And I get invitations to events and projects because I'm a Bram Stoker Award winner or a Scribe Award winner or a New York Times bestseller. Does that mean my works are substantially better than someone who does not have these milestone credits? Not at all. But because publishing is a business it would be poor business practice not to use the tools at one's disposal.

I also sit on juries for various groups (Mystery Writers of America, Horror Writers Association, etc.) to judge works in categories where I do not currently publish. This affords me the opportunity to read a lot of the best works, and to discover works I might otherwise not have had the good fortune to read.

KNOST: What marketing elements (that work well for you) do you think most authors overlook?

MABERRY: I often meet writers who say that they 'hate Twitter' or 'hate Facebook' and essentially turn thumbs down on social media as a time-wasting nothing. They are mistaken. Used correctly, social media is the single strongest tool for brand management (and remember, the writer is the brand) and marketing. People who don't know this most likely simply don't know how best to utilize these tools. They can learn. They should learn.

KNOST: Knowing what you know now, what marketing aspects would you focus on heavily if you were starting out in the business today?

Michael Knost

MABERRY: Social media is the core marketing tool in this digital age. Nothing else comes close. There are some things more satisfying -- in-person gatherings of writers, public appearances, and so on -- but they don't have the scope of social media. Someone just starting out needs to build a social media presence, and establish their brand, even before they have a product on the market. They need to connect with other people who enjoy the genre in which the writer plans to publish. They need to connect with other writers, readers, bloggers, reviewers, librarians, booksellers, and fans. Lots of fans. When I had my first thriller coming out (PATIENT ZERO), I friended other writers in my genre, the bloggers who were reviewing books by those writers, and the most active fans of those writers. I joined the conversation and I didn't try to hijack the conversation to make it about me. I became part of the community of people who dig that genre. I posted links to new books and movies. I posted favorable reviews. I slammed nothing. Ever. Why? Because negativity doesn't sell product and it closes doors. When my own book came out, I used a subtle hand in promoting it. My social media posts -- except on release day -- are generally NOT about my books. They are about pop culture with a bias toward my genre. New writers should dive into the social media waters and learn how to swim as soon as they can.

KNOST: How important (as a promising novelist) is it marketing wise to publish short stories or non-fiction in many magazines and anthologies?

MABERRY: Publishing short fiction allows a lot of people to gain exposure to your works. It's a sampler. And, when you're starting out you'll often be in anthologies or magazines with bigger names. That's great. The readers will be drawn to those heavy hitters, but they will find your works. That's terrific exposure and, to some degree, it validates you by being in the same book as them.

Also, writing short fiction allows for experimentation. I've written short stories that are way outside of my comfort zone. Stuff I would probably never have tried. But those experiments allow you to stretch and grow as a writer. My whole YA career came out of a novella I was asked to write for Christopher Golden's The New Dead zombie anthology. I would never have written that story otherwise. While writing that story, "The Family Business", I discovered a whole new cast of characters and a setting that opened a door into young adult fiction. I later expanded that story into the novel, Rot & Ruin, which has gone on to become an international bestselling series of novels, as well as comics and a movie now in development. And I did a Wizard of Oz story for one of John Joseph Adam's anthologies, Oz Reimagined. Instead of writing a gritty horror story set in Oz, I instead experimented with a gentle fable, "The Cobbler of Oz", which was so well-received that it has been included in the official Chronology of Oz. So...yeah, short stories are great in many, many ways.

Nonfiction is useful, too. I started out as a nonfiction magazine feature writer, and later I wrote textbooks and mass market nonfiction books. I learned a lot of useful skills, particularly in understand the market, structural logic, research and so on. And my nonfiction book on the folklore of the supernatural, The Vampire Slayers Field Guide to the Undead (written under the pen name of Shane MacDougall), led me to try my hand at writing my first fiction, the vampire novel, Ghost Road Blues.

KNOST: What precautions do you take to protect your name brand?

MABERRY: For me brand is about integrity and attitude. I used to be a very negative person and then I discovered that negativity is a self-tightening knot. It doesn't do you a damn bit of good. So I shifted to focusing on the positive elements of my writing and my career. I looked for, and found, the things about writing and publishing that were fun and uplifting. I reached out to do a lot of community building among writers. I stayed out of fights. I decided to never post negative comments or reviews (I'm a writer, not a critic) and to be a cheerleader for the success of other writers. The result is that I established a brand of an affable guy who is professional and compassionate, but one who is savvy in business and supportive of others. That's a brand that makes you want to smile at yourself in the shaving mirror. It makes you feel like you are contributing something to the writing world rather than feeding off of it. And, it's an infectious thing. People want to be happy and writers -- despite the mystique of the brooding artist -- do their best work when they are not depressed, angry, or resentful.

This kind of brand takes management. I make sure that the stuff I post on Facebook and other social media reflects and supports that brand. I don't get bitchy and I don't take cheap shots. I also invite my fellow creative types to share in their success by starting threads where they can take about their current work in progress, or their career milestones. And when I'm speaking to groups of writers -- such as at writers conferences or in my monthly free Writers Coffeehouse networking sessions—I encourage them to build brands that are a balance of fun and professional.

KNOST: How important are book signing events and personal appearances?

MABERRY: Sadly, with the decline of the number of brick-and-mortar bookstores, signings have become less of an effective tool. They are often costly for the store and unless they are a well-attended runaway hit they can create a feeling of frustration for many writers. That said, bookstore appearances still have their place and a writer should get behind the promotional wagon and push to make those events successful.

I love doing bookstore events. I try not to flood the local stores, though, because that dilutes the sales potential for each store. And events like readings, Q&A, and panels tend to draw bigger crowds, which are better for everyone.

Most of the public appearances I do are at conventions. I am a total panel junkie, and a good panel is not only gobs of fun, it sells books, too. And appearances at conventions puts you in front of a lot of folks who may not yet know who you are. You have a chance to wow them and connect with them. And you get to meet them!

KNOST: What marketing mistakes have you made that you learned from?

MABERRY: If there are fifty things you can do wrong, I did all fifty and then added some points to the list. But I take those as learning experiences. I used to have a negative vibe, but I learned from how that played out. I discovered that having fun works better. I also made mistakes early on by focusing only on the craft side of writing and not bothering (despite the advice I got from Ray Bradbury

and Richard Matheson) to learn the nuts and bolts of the publishing side of things. That was a mistake, and it cost me. But I learned from it and as a result my business acumen has been every bit as important as my writing craftsmanship in building a successful career. Luckily this is a model everyone else can copy!

PURCHASING ADVERTISING

We want our work to be seen and to be read, right? As writers, our marketing plans can be as big or as small as we want. We can choose to write great fiction and never worry about promoting our art, or we can work our tails (or tales if you prefer) off as sales professionals, pushing our products like car salesmen -- I'm sure you know there are thousands of levels in between.

No matter what you are willing to strive for, I suggest you have a plan.

Regardless of the level you are comfortable with in marketing yourself and/or your wares, you need a plan to help you achieve success.

Failing to plan = planning to fail.

This could be as simple as setting up book signings or appearances, or as elaborate as purchasing advertising in magazines, newspapers, radio, and television. Having a plan will help you stay on track. As creative people, we tend to have short attention spans. We get started on something, focusing our attention to the smallest of details ... and then we get excited about something else and tend to forget about the first things we started, or ignore them to make time for the newest idea.

Since I talked about free and cheap marketing ideas earlier, I'd like to talk about how to get more bangs for your bucks should you decide to purchase advertising out of your own pocket. There are three things to keep in mind:

You Need to Reach the Right Audience

Let's say your new book is about satanic worship with an anti-religious theme. You certainly wouldn't want to purchase advertising on the local Christian radio station, now would you? The people who listen to that radio station are more than likely not your target audience.

That's fairly obvious, but it can be drilled down even more with a bit of research. For instance, if you could market the same book on a cable television network, making sure your commercials are scheduled to air during similar shows would mean you are going to hit more of your target audience than you would if you scheduled the ads to run during Antiques Roadshow. Now, don't get me wrong, I am not saying people who watch Antiques Roadshow would not be interested in a satanic worship novel, but we can pretty much agree you would find more of your audience watching The Walking Dead.

When you talk to sales associates from varying media outlets, be sure to ask them for help in researching their product. Many of them use ratings services that can tell you which shows or times or networks would be best according to the information they have available from service diaries, etc. If you want to reach males ages 25 to 40 who earn more than $35,000 per year and live within a thirty-mile radius of you, the salesperson can do it with just a few clicks on the computer.

If it's newspaper, where is the best place for your ad to appear? Maybe the research shows more of your target reads the obituary page, and they have retention rates of ads they saw when the ads are placed above the fold, which means on the top half of the newspaper page.

Do your research, find where your target spends the majority of their time and plan to spend the majority of your advertising dollars there.

You Need to Deliver the Right Message

The next thing you need to do is deliver the right message. Sounds easy enough, huh? Well, it's not as simple as it sometimes looks. The first thing I would suggest is to find out what your U.S.P (Unique Selling Proposition) is. In other words, what makes you or your product stand out from your competitor?

If you ran a pizza shop in a town where there are twenty other pizza shops, what makes you different from the others? Maybe you are the only shop that offers free delivery. If so, that is a great Unique Selling Proposition.

What is it about your book that makes it different than others? Find that and focus on it. Focus on one thing in your ad. Don't water down your message with too much for the reader/listener/viewer to digest. The more products you push, the fewer your potential customer will retain your information. They will experience tune out. You become just another noise in the background of life.

I'll give you a good example of this. What is it that Geico Insurance focuses on in their commercials? They focus on a number of things, but only one thing in each commercial. One commercial may push motorcycle insurance, one may push boat insurance, one may push RV insurance, but you won't see one pushing all three ... unless they are pushing a special policy for all three that will save you more if you bundle all three. And they almost always all end with the same tagline. "Geico: Just 15 minutes could save you 15% or more."

You Need Continuity

After you know your target audience, and know your message, you need to make sure you keep the same message everywhere you advertise. What I mean by this is if you purchase advertising at a few radio stations, a few television stations, and a few newspapers and magazines, all your commercials or ads should focus on the same message. The same theme, product, and message should be identical across the board.

If you can use the same voice from radio in your television ads, do it ... you might even be able to use the exact audio from radio as the audio for the television producers to produce the images around your televised commercial. The same images and fonts and themes should be used in all your print ads, and they should reflect your web presence, too.

You can go further, but if you use these as the basic bones, you will be far ahead of the others trying to compete with you in professional media.

TELEVISION ADVERTISING

Yes, so many advertising dollars have been shifted to digital or Internet markets these days in every industry. However, terrestrial radio, periodicals, and television are still viable channels to put to use. I plan to cover all three in this book, but I want to start with television. First came newspapers, then came radio, and television followed. Since then, the digital age has exploded, introducing us to everything from advertising on the Internet to advertising on satellite radio or television.

According to a recent study by Ball State University on the media consumption habits of average Americans, despite the Internet's steady rise in popularity over the last several years, television remains the dominant medium in most U.S. households. On average, the general population spends over four and a half hours a day in front of the tube, making TV viewing one of the most common modern leisure activities.

But, television, like all other traditional outlets, is battling the digital age. Not only do we as consumers have online sources like Netflix, Hulu, and Amazon, making it possible to cheaply stream movies and shows, we also have digital DVRs, Tivo units, and smart televisions. We also have set top boxes for streaming content, which can access digital radio, music, movies, shows, etc.

Before you choose which is best for you, you need to understand your target demographic and then research accordingly. Now, many television companies will be more than happy to help you research! In fact, every one of them will have data to prove they are the best option.

The first thing you have to do is view everything through your skeptical sunglasses. Ask for specifics. You want Arbitron or Scarborough or Nielson ratings for the demographic you hope to reach. So, if it is adults between 25 and 55 with a household income of $70,000 or more, they can print out all the data to show you where they stand, and where the competitors stand with that demo.

Now, you should be mindful of two different animals here when it comes to ratings and numbers. First of all, a television show can get high ratings nationally, yet air on a local station that has a very poor viewership. So, knowing the national rating for a particular show is good, but the most important thing for you is how are the ratings for the local station and show on that station? That's why local ratings are so vital to regional marketing.

When it comes to traditional television, you have broadcast and cable.

Broadcast television is a local station -- generally a media affiliate of a larger company like NBC or CBS. These stations can provide coverage maps, showing you how far they reach while broadcasting a signal in the geographic area you want to focus on.

Broadcast stations have original programming like news, weather, etc., which usually delivers big numbers. These stations also carry shows and programs from the network they are affiliated with. So, if the station is an NBC affiliate, it will air most all programs NBC offers. And because it is a broadcast station, it will cover a lot of area, which can be good, as well as bad. I'll get into that in a minute.

Cable television does not broadcast a signal. Cable television is basically an enormous server that distributes content to subscribers. When you sign up for cable, you are getting a line to the server for the programming.

Cable television is not limited to airing programs from just one network. Some networks have affiliate broadcast stations, but not the majority. NBC, CBS, ABC, FOX, CW, PBS are just a few that do. Networks like CNN, Comedy Central, SyFy, and HBO do not. Therefore, these networks distribute their programming via cable networks.

Broadcast television can be more expensive because of its broad reach, whereas cable typically allows you to buy (much cheaper) commercial time for a specific zone of a larger market. For instance, let's say you want to advertise a book on the history of a small town in your state. Lets say the broadcast station you are interested in has a reach that includes the small town, but it also includes the entire state.

Cable advertising can reach that specific audience without making you pay for areas unlikely to be interested. Broadcast TV forces you to buy the entire market. That gives you more eyeballs, and if your business draws traffic from your entire metropolitan area you'll want that extra exposure, but if not, keep in mind that you're paying for an audience you may not need.

However, although a local broadcast station may be on a cable network, you can't purchase advertising in the local station via the cable company. The same goes with satellite television. However, if you purchase advertising on a local broadcast station, more than likely your ads will be seen on cable and satellite television, as the local networks are usually included in the basic packages.

Now, let's talk about your commercials. You can run thirty-second spots or fifteen-second spots. You can expect greater rates of viewer recall by running what is known as bookends, which are two fifteen-second spots—one running at the beginning of the commercial break and the second one running at the end of the break.

You can also expect higher rates of viewer recall when your commercials have production treatments or affective appeals that are congruent with that of the programming within which they are placed.

One of my publishers actually put out a few of the books that were used as reference material for the Hatfields and McCoys miniseries on the History Channel a few years ago. I suggested he contact the local cable company and see if he could get a package deal to run spots promoting the books in our local area, which is the regional area where the famous feud actually transpired.

He ended up getting several commercials aired during the show and many bonus spots outside the show for just a few hundred bucks ... and the sales of those books went through the roof.

You want to make sure the spot is simple with a clear message. A good commercial does not have to be funny or hard sell or artsy to be effective. It just needs to do exactly what you want it to do. But, you do want quality, so you may spend some bucks on getting it produced by a professional.

Now, many folks think that television commercials are not as effective in this day and time because of DVRs and Tivo, where the viewer can fast-forward past the commercials to quickly return to the programming. However, studies have shown that viewer recall is usually higher in DVR and Tivo playback, especially because of fast-forwarding. As it turns out, the viewer is more attentive to what is playing at this time than with most all other television viewing habits.

And for this very reason, when producing a television commercial, make sure you have a static graphic at the bottom or top that maintains your logo and website or name or phone number throughout the entire spot. Because even during the high speed fast-forwarding, the viewer will read and recognize the elements you want to get across via that static image.

But, before you go out and purchase advertising, be sure to do your research. Also, make sure you understand exactly what your goal is. Then, create the simplest message you can for the viewer to fully understand what it is you are asking them to do.

RADIO ADVERTISING

Where television offers the viewer visual and audio, very little is left to the imagination. I think this is why books and radio are so much alike.

I worked in the radio industry for over twenty years, starting out as a part time disc jockey and working my way up to program director, sales director, and then general manager.

Just as in books, radio sparks the Theater of the Mind, allowing the reader or listener to be an active participant. You can't physically see a character in the book as you can with movies or television -- and you can't physically see the characters in the radio commercial. So, Theater of the Mind begins producing those images. And when that happens, it is powerful because no movie director or cinematographer can produce images as detailed or as beautiful as our own imagination can.

For the same reason you don't always offer non-essential descriptive details (eye color, hair color, height, etc.) in your stories when those details have nothing to do with moving the story forward, you do the same in radio advertising. Because the more you allow the reader/listener to fill in the blanks, the more connected they are to the story or commercial or event. In a sense, they become a co-writer of sorts -- you give all the necessary details and the reader/listener fills in the rest.

The cool thing, however, is in radio, instead of telling us the sounds you want to convey, you can actually show them. Instead of telling us a car door slams, you can insert the sound effect of a car door slamming. That sound will initiate the Theater of the Mind to not only visualize the whole thing, but will put the listener inside the car. Use this to your advantage.

When it comes to radio station numbers, there are several ways to measure radio audiences. The data from diaries is converted into several types of audience measure, each of which is useful for a different purpose. The main measures are:

• Average Audience

• Reach, or Cumulative Audience

• Share

• Duration

• Impressions

• Frequency - Average and Distribution

• Loyalty

Average audience

The average audience is simply the average number of people listening to a particular station in a particular time period. This is usually expressed as estimated thousands of listeners, but sometimes as a percentage of the relevant population.

The time period can be:

- A quarter-hour,

- A time zone - which can be defined in any way, but often corresponds to one program segment, of several hours,

- A whole day - sometimes excluding any hours when the station is not on air,

- A week

These average audience figures can be calculated for any demographic group.

Reach

The reach of a radio station, also known as *cumulative audience,* is the number of different people who listen to a station in a time period longer than the basic unit. If the basic unit is a quarter-hour, then the reach for a quarter-hour is the same as the average. As the time period grows, the reach grows, too, but more and more slowly.

Share

Audience share is a different kind of measure altogether. Both average audience and reach are counts of people. Audience share, though always expressed as a percentage, is not a percentage of people, but of person-hours. Take the statement "Rock 105 has a 40% share of the radio audience in this area." That means: out of every 100 hours that people in the area spend listening to radio, Rock 105 has 40 of those hours. That does not mean it has a reach of 40%.

Duration of listening

Duration is sometimes known as the *average time spent listening (TSL)*, which describes it clearly. Obviously, the longer listeners spend listening, the more chances your commercial will be heard. It also means more impressions (I'll explain that in a second). And this all means better retention rates.

Impressions

Impressions, also known as *impacts,* is a measure used by advertisers. It's the sum of the audiences at specified times - e.g. when ads are broadcast. If a station has an audience of 2,000 in one quarter-hour and 2,500 in the next, and the same ad is broadcast once in each quarter hour, that will be 4,500 impressions: the number of times the ad was heard, regardless of the number of different people who heard it.

Frequency

Frequency is another measure used mainly in advertising. It's an answer to the question, "How often did listeners hear the ad?" If an ad is broadcast twice in each of two quarter-hours, the frequency will range between 0 (because some people will not have heard it at all) and 4 (among those who listened to the station for both quarter-hours). Actually, there are two measures of frequency: the *average frequency* and the *frequency distribution.* Frequency is normally based on the whole population -- because that's who the advertiser is trying to attract. If we know that the reach for the two quarter-hours was 3,000, and that there were 9,000 impressions, the average frequency must be 3. A full frequency distribution would show how many people heard the ad four times, three times, twice, once, and not at all.

Loyalty

If all listeners to a station listen only to that station, its loyalty is 100%. This is usually measured over one week: a standard cycle time in radio listening, both for programming and for survey samples. By definition, loyalty cannot be zero: listeners to a station must spend *some* time listening to it, otherwise they wouldn't qualify as listeners. So the formula for loyalty to station A is: (time spent listening to station A) divided (by time spent listening to all stations)...usually expressed as a percentage. In an area with between about 5 and 20 stations available, a loyalty figure of 50% is on the high side. In other words, if the people who listen to your station at least once a week spend more time with your station than with all others combined, you are doing well.

Your spot placement in a break matters

Studies have shown you can expect higher rates of listener recall with commercials that run second in the commercial break. Yes, many think the first commercial going into the break is the best, others think it is the last, but the truth of the matter is it is the second spot in the break. There are many factors that play into this, but it does work. I have tested it myself in focus groups. I am always amazed at the results.

Have a single goal in mind when you advertise

Maybe you want to sell more copies of your latest book. Maybe you want more traffic and awareness of your website. Maybe you want to promote a writer workshop you are teaching. There is a slim chance you will ever hit your target if you do not take time to aim at it.

Focus your commercial on one thing

Is that a book? Is that your website? Is that you as an author? Is that a specific event? Keep the focus on one thing. So, don't promote all your books ... focus on one. Don't focus on all your events for a particular month ... focus on one.

The rule of threes applies in radio advertising, too

Therefore, try to mention the one thing you want to promote three times. However, you want to do it in a creative way so it doesn't come across as monotonous.

Make your message relevant and about the listener

By creating a message that's relevant to your target demo's life, they'll create an interest in your commercial, and want to know more. Once you get a listener *wanting* to learn about your product or service, their minds are open to absorb information, and you can brand your company's name into their long-term memory. Illustrate the experience of using your product, show how your service benefits them, and use terms and concepts that paint a picture. If listeners can see it in their life, they'll create a need for it. If you start an ad only with information about your company, you may lose the listener before they even realize they want what you sell. Give them a relevant reason to care about you first.

Make your message interesting and hard to ignore

A common ad is a common mistake. When creating, don't fall into the trap of worrying about what a radio ad should or typically sounds like. Try to avoid being like others. If your commercial has unique elements, it'll stand out in the commercial clutter and make people curious to learn more. If it's filled with common clichés and generalities, not many will remember it. Since today's consumers are hit by over 5000 advertisements a day (signs, television, online, etc.), you really need to be different to make an impact. Find one or two really interesting and beneficial points, and don't let people ignore the message, or even worse forget it. But how do you avoid being ignored? Be entertaining, make an interesting point, tell a story, be anything but the usual!

Use a unique voice

Far too often, local station personalities voice 85% of all commercials on their stations. If you allow one of these people to voice your commercial, you are taking a chance at your spot being lost in the sea of familiar voices. Instead, find a unique voice (maybe yours if you are professional enough) to stand out in the crowd. There are far too many voiceover talents out there for you to take advantage of and not have your commercial sound like everyone else's.

I highly recommend John DeVincent. John has been in the radio industry for years, and has served as creative director for some very large broadcast companies. You will get the highest of quality with a unique voice with John, and you will get what you ask for in the time you need it.

His email is john@johndevincent.com and his website

is www.johndevincent.com. Tell him Michael Knost sent you. He's a great guy, and he is a writer, too, so, he knows where you are coming from.

Make your message simple and clear

Many ads out there are too complex. Being too clever can sometimes go over the listener's head and they'll never remember it. Or promoting too much information that distracts or bores them can lose them. You can't expect a person that has work, family, health, daily chores, errands, street signs, etc. on their minds, to figure out a complex message. Narrow down what you want to say to only the most compelling point(s), and keep it simple. Repeating the main point is also never a bad thing. While it may sound redundant to you (the business who's close to the product) consumers can sometimes need reassurance of what they just heard is correct. If it's clear how your business can help the consumer, simplicity will help you be Top Of Mind. Help the listener, don't outsmart them.

Define your Unique Selling Proposition

Your Unique Selling Proposition (USP) is what makes your business different from everyone else in your market. For example, (as I mentioned earlier) if your pizza shop is the only one in town that delivers, that is a great USB. Be sure to give the listener your unique selling proposition in the commercial.

Examples:

Domino's Pizza -- *You get fresh, hot pizza delivered to your door in 30-minutes or less or it's free.*

FedEx -- *When it absolutely, positively has to be there overnight.*

GEICO -- *15 Minutes Could Save You 15% or More on Car Insurance.*

Simply stated, your Unique Selling Proposition is a summary of what makes your business unique and valuable to your target market. It answers the question: How does your services or products benefit your clients better than your competitor's services or products?

Radio advertising works if you make sure all the details are covered. So, give it a shot sometime and get tuned in for the results!

NEWSPAPER ADVERTISING

Often cheaper than broadcast advertising, newspaper advertising usually provides advantages of greater market share in many locations. Also, newspaper marketing does not depend on the target audience having a television or radio on at a certain time in order to receive the message of the advertisement.

Newspaper advertising comes in two formats: display or classified. Display ads are those that span multiple columns horizontally and often include graphics and borders. Classified advertising is in-column advertising that follows the natural flow of the column down the page vertically.

Classified advertising is usually the cheapest option for most people and appeals to those who are after a certain market. For example, those seeking to rent an apartment, find a job, or buy a pet typically use classified ads to aid in their searching. Although not traditional to classified ads, many publications offer small graphics and borders with classified ads. Classified ads are usually found in a specific section.

Display ads are generally higher profile ads that take up, in many cases, significant portions of the page. Typically, display ads may take up an eighth, quarter, half, or full page. In some cases, the ad may take up two facing pages (these are known as Double Truck ads), those ads are rare in newspaper advertising simply because of the cost. Display ads may either be in color or black and white, with the color option costing more.

In many cases, newspapers offer services to advertisers to help them design effective display pieces. In all cases, the advertiser has the right to refuse or accept this service.

In a relatively new development, some newspapers offer a package of advertising that not only includes newspaper advertising but online advertising on the newspaper's website as well. This helps alleviate fears among some advertisers that their target audience may not be reading the newspaper, but simply going online. Most newspapers that have websites offer some sort of online advertising in addition to their newspaper advertising, though not all publications package the two together.

Placement Recommendations

Purchasing advertising in a newspaper without negotiating placement lets the layout artist or the advertising sales manager put your ad where he or she feels it belongs. And more than likely, they are just looking for the most convenient spot to stick it in. Because those people don't always have your best interests in mind or understand what you're trying to accomplish, you should set a few rules for where your ad will run as part of your contract.

Choose a Right-Hand Page

The eye naturally travels from left-to-right when viewing a page with text, starting at the top left of the page and moving downward to the right. For this reason, many savvy advertisers ask for what is called right-reading page placement, with the ad placed on the bottom, right-hand side of the right page. Include this placement in your contract and make sure you are not charged extra for this.

Choose Your Section

Newspapers are often published in sections, such as sports, business, cooking and real estate. While you might think the paper will naturally place you in the section most closely associated with your business, that's not always the case, so request placement in the section where you want the ad to run. Consider the maker of women's fitness apparel who wants its ad placed in the parenting section to be seen by young mothers rather than amid other apparel ads in the paper's health and fitness section. The newspaper would not know this advertiser's strategy if it wasn't told. And, just so you know, a couple of great sections to advertise books in are Lifestyles as well as Entertainment.

Review Editorial Content

Consider the Fold

Advertising is placed above or below the fold, or on the top or bottom half of the page when the paper is folded. This is similar to a website page, with ads running at the top of the page commanding a higher premium because they are seen immediately and not missed if readers don't scroll down the page. Discuss with your sales reps whether or not being above or below the fold is better for a certain page or section.

Analyze Days

Some newspapers run sections once a week or cater to

a particular audience on a specific day. Some papers let subscribers purchase two- or three-day subscriptions, for example. And many foodies focus on Wednesday's paper when supermarkets traditionally use inserts, offer specials or include coupons. Ask your sales rep to tell you what day of the week is best to reach your target audience.

Know the Costs

Even if your ad sales rep wants to do a good job for you and gives you what she feels is a prime spot, she might put your ad somewhere that doesn't further your goals. Before you ask for your ad to appear in a specific area of a newspaper, review your contract to determine if there is an extra charge for preferred space. Some contracts give the paper control over where your ad will run, charging you an extra fee for guaranteed placement. An advertising sales rep might include preferred or guaranteed placement in your contract at no extra charge to get your business.

Mistakes To Avoid When Designing Your Newspaper Ad

Here are some mistakes to avoid when designing for newspapers along with some other tips.

• Too much clutter. Don't forget the importance of white space. If you can't fit in all the information you had hoped to, consider going with a larger ad, or editing down your information to a more manageable amount, or get creative... how can you say your whole message in just a few words or a picture? Hey, you're a writer, you should be able to do this with ease!

• Unclear message. Make sure you know what you are trying to get your reader to do before you start to design your ad. Keep this objective in mind at all times and review your ad when you are done to make sure this has been accomplished.

• Errors. Even though it may seem easy to proofread such a small set of type, sometimes errors show up and are glossed over no matter how many times you read it. To be safe, have someone else review your ad for you also ... this goes with almost all graphic design work. Again, you're an author, you should be used to this anyway.

• Lack of contact information. This common error is particularly frustrating for readers. You may have convinced your reader to contact you or purchase your products, but if they can't easily find contact information, they will probably not bother to look much further. Always have a call to action.

• AIDA. Try to remember this acronym ... AIDA. Attention, Information, Desire, Action. Get the reader's attention, give them the information and desire for your product, then give them a call to action.

I wish I had a dollar for every time I have heard someone say advertising does not work. The truth is advertising is a multi-billion dollar industry and that would not be the case if it did not work. Advertising can work for your business, you just need to be good at it and you need to do it consistently.

Like most marketing, it can be done well or badly. The

secret is to test, test, and test again. Test what? Test your headlines, copy, use of pictures, location, offer, use of color, typeface, the special offer you make, the size of your advert, and even the location of your telephone number.

Oh, and one of the best things about paid advertisement is that as a client to the newspaper, you sort of get preferential treatment when it comes to free publicity and press releases. So, don't be afraid to get your advertising campaigns underway.

MAGAZINE ADVERTISING

Most of the advertising mediums we have covered so far have focused on geographical marketing -- radio, newspapers, and television. These mediums broadcast or publish within a specific location, so the marketing efforts are spent on reaching a broadly defined demographic. But, I'd like to put some spotlight on an advertising medium that focuses on what I call Appeal Marketing. I'm talking about magazine advertising.

Appeal marketing is a form of niche marketing. It just means instead of shooting for potential customers according to age group, gender, geography, or other factors, you are targeting potential customer's with specific interests. Now, don't get me wrong, you can cover broad reach via magazine marketing as well, but most magazines cover some type of niche interest. And that's what makes appeal marketing so powerful.

There are magazines covering nearly every genre you can imagine. Some of these magazines publish short fiction, and some only focus on movies, television shows, non-fiction, etc. Let's say you write in the horror field. There are a number of magazines in the genre you could consider advertising in -- a few of them even publish short fiction. So, this means the people purchasing the magazine are more than likely the most perfect target audience you can find. After all, they are purchasing those magazines to read horror fiction. Therefore, advertising in niche periodicals is such a fantastic idea.

However, one of the things you need to keep in mind when it comes to advertising in magazines as opposed to advertising in radio, television, or newspapers, you are looking at advance time that is far greater than anything else that you have experienced.

For instance, with radio, you can have a commercial on the air in the same day you purchased the advertising. You can be on the air almost as quickly as when the spot is ready. So, if you could get a spot quickly recorded, make the order, within minutes (on most stations) your commercial will be airing.

Newspaper has a little longer prep time. Don't ever think you will get an ad in in the same day. I would go as far as to say don't even expect to get an ad in the next day with most newspapers. There are two factors to newspaper advertising you need to consider: first, is scheduling and the second is production.

Sure, your spots need to be scheduled in radio, too, but the deejay working can hand-write where he played the spots on the log for the traffic director to adjust and bill. Newspaper is different because ads are scheduled ahead of time like a jigsaw puzzle. How much room they have for other content is going to depend on how much advertisement is scheduled. And if the ad is not scheduled ahead of time, there will be no room to put it. So, schedule times will be different with every newspaper because some are daily newspapers and some are weeklies.

Television prep time is often longer than newspaper. Much of the time production is the culprit in this medium rather than schedule like newspaper, although schedule will have to be made early as well -- most often a week or two ahead of time. But, production generally takes so much longer for television than production for newspaper or radio. Give yourself at least a week for production time. So, production and scheduling is going to take up weeks of prep time.

But, you can expect things to be quite different when advertising for magazines. Generally speaking, you can expect up to a several month prep time for many magazines. Most of them have everything scheduled and planned so far out in order to get production streamlined that in most cases many magazines are working on the December issue in July. Now, it may not be that far ahead in some of the smaller magazines, but it would be smart for you to think ahead and contact any of the magazines you intend to use in the near future.

It's important to make your contacts and get a feel for the numbers as soon as possible. I say this because this is one medium you can't just decide to advertise in by the seat of your pants and expect to get in. Thinking ahead is required to make solid decisions when advertising in periodicals. Don't get me wrong, sometimes other advertisers have to pull out for reasons beyond them and you may luck out and get a slot, but the chances of that are very slim.

Let's say you have a book that is going to hit bookshelves in October, then you should start planning and scheduling at least several months ahead. The earliest you can do it, contact the magazine about what they have available. Then go ahead and schedule. Don't think everything is clear and you can wait until later to schedule, because the avails can be depleted within a few days in July for the October issue. When you contact the magazine in July, go ahead and schedule.

Now, keep in mind, this doesn't mean you have to have your copy ready. You won't need to send your ad to them until later. You just need to schedule. It's the same as setting up a hotel reservation -- you don't have to pack your bags at the same time you make the reservation six-months ahead. You may have to pay for the ad upfront, but at least you know it is scheduled and will run when you want it to run. Then you have months to have the ad produced. And you may need that time because the publisher has yet to give you all the details you need like the ISBN number, final title, the final book cover, and the exact date the book will hit bookshelves.

There are many options to consider when purchasing magazine advertising. Does the magazine have some pages slick-stock and some a variant grade? Do they offer full color or spot color or just black and white? Check on the pricing for each. Don't take for granted the price you get is going to include color. You need to ask.

There are different sizes of ads to choose from. You don't want something too small, but you may not want to break the bank by going full page either. So, a good balance between size and price will come into play.

I suggest you consider if you plan to run the ad just once, or do you think you may run it for three months or six months. Because, if you know you will run it for six months, you should talk to the magazine about getting a discount for running multiple times. You can save a great deal of money just by doing so. Honestly, if you are going to run that many regardless, why not save hundreds of dollars?

A great side effect of advertising extensively with magazines is you can expect a few perks that you never expected before. The biggest being you will see the magazine will now be more open to reviewing your books than they were before. Now, that doesn't mean they will give you positive reviews, and you should not expect them to do so just because you are advertising with them. In fact, you should not even expect them to review your works because you advertise with them.

In marketing and advertising there is a term that many use called Top Mind Awareness. It means you saturate the market with advertising so consistently that when listeners/viewers/readers are in need of a product you provide, you come to mind first. Top Mind Awareness also works when it comes to name branding for authors. When you advertise in magazines and trade publications, your name is branding the minds of readers, authors, editors, publishers, and agents. This means your name brand grows.

Which is why a high quality ad is imperative. You need to hire a graphic artist that will help you make an impression. Remember what I said about not letting radio personalities of local stations voice your commercials because their voice is so common with listeners the voices cause tune--out? Your commercial doesn't stand out, it's just another commercial in the sea of sameness. Which is why you hire a voiceover talent who is not already on the station ... this voice belongs to you exclusively.

You want to do the same with a graphic artist in magazine ads. You don't want one of the magazine's graphic artists to produce your ad, as the ads all look the same -- they have the same voice. That's why hiring a professional graphic artist will make your ad stand out from everyone else's. However, if you can't afford to go with a professional that is not affiliated with the magazine, and the magazine offers free or cheap production, take them up on it instead of trying to do your own ad. I can't stress enough how important quality is in this matter.

Last thing I want you to think about is this: it's called Appeal Marketing for a reason. You are focusing on a target that finds a specific interest appealing. Which means reading fiction, or science fiction, or romance, or fantasy. You should align your advertising to the appeal. "If you are a fan of Stephen King, you will love … " is a headline that will help align you with most horror fans.

Use quotes from blurbs you've received from well-known writers in the field in the ad. Because a blurb is an endorsement from a proven professional in the genre most fans will know and love. It's like finding acceptance with a group of people because one of the popular one's has vouched for you, or has introduced you to everyone.

Just remember to appeal to what appeals to the reader when focusing on appeal marketing.

OUTDOOR ADVERTISING

Advertising might be a changing industry, but it is still important as ever to make your business' name known to potential customers. There are many different types of outdoor advertising that have unique advantages and disadvantages. Depending on what kind of product is being sold and the message the business wants to get across will determine the best choice of outdoor advertising.

While there are many differences in types of outdoor advertising, there are some common advantages versus online and TV advertising. Both forms are useful in their own way, but it is important to understand the differences to make a more informed choice. Here are several forms of outdoor advertising and how they provide unique benefits:

Billboards and Street Signs

Billboard advertising is one of the oldest forms of advertising and remains strong today. There have been some innovations in the market with the invention of digital billboards run with LCD or plasma screens. Traditional billboards are still highly used and prove to be an effective form of advertising. In general, billboards can be a great way to advertise for businesses that are interested in growing brand awareness and brand recognition.

Many businesses use billboards to get a message across or to raise awareness of their name brand. However, if you notice, there are a lot more business types that do not use them. And there is a reason for this. Yes, billboards can raise awareness of the name brand, especially so when used in conjunction with other advertising means -- as in, radio, television, in newspapers. But, billboards serve one function very well, and that is what I call DIRECTIONAL. The best utilization of the billboard, or the best example of the best utilization of the billboard would be those you see on highways or roads directing you to something on that road. For instance, McDonald's is on the next exit.

But, with billboards the rule of thumb is to not exceed seven words. Yeah, and you thought Twitter was hard to do anything with 140 characters! But, think about it, someone driving past a billboard on a highway will not be reading paragraphs of verbiage. And this is one of the reasons billboards are a tough sell to many businesses.

• Benefits of Highway Billboards - Highway billboards are great for businesses like hotels, convenience stores and gas stations, and fast food. When people travel, billboards are one of the ways that people search for a place to eat or rest for the night.

• Benefits of Digital Billboards - Digital billboards are great for businesses that don't have a large budget. Digital billboards are inexpensive because the price is divided among many different companies making the cost lower for each advertiser.

• Benefits of Local Billboards - Local billboards are

posted around town and are good for businesses that serve a specific geographic region like handyman services, insurance and tax professionals, and many more. There is a wide variety of businesses that can benefit from these and there might be high competition for any given position.

Car Magnets and Body Wraps

Car magnets and body wraps are a form of outdoor advertising that are really useful for businesses that use cars and trucks as an essential part of their process. Examples would be a food delivery service, maintenance trucks, moving trucks, and others. Magnets are less expensive and easier to apply, but are not as visible as body wraps. Body wraps are paint jobs or a series of graphics printed on adhesive vinyl that display an advertisement on every side of the car.

These could serve you as an author as you pull into a particular event. It could also serve well if you in the parking lot of a library, bookstore, or convention. It is advertising as people walk by, heading inside.

Bus and Rail

Bus and rail advertising is ideal for local business located close to one of these transportation stops. Both forms get significant traffic, especially in larger, densely populated areas. However, depending on your target demographic, bus shelter advertising and rail station advertisements can also be used to increase brand recognition through repetition.

Many commuters use the same routes daily and will be exposed to an advertisement on multiple occasions. Also, metropolitan areas often have a lot of tourists and business people traveling in and out using public transportation, providing a perfect opportunity to reach that market.

These are fantastic areas to advertise your book. Imagine your book cover everywhere. And you would be surprised at how cheap these ads can be. Don't be afraid to check them out.

One could also include tee-shirts, ink pens, and other items that will display your name or book in the public. Remember to include your web URL and book covers or titles.

BOOK TRAILERS

"I'm interested in book trailer videos. Who makes them?
What does it cost to have them made? And what else
comes with the territory of having them made?"
— Rob Darnell, Lapeer, MI.

Much like movie trailers advertising the latest blockbuster film that is coming to a theater near you, book trailers are short video commercials introducing your book to potential readers. There are differences, however, and you need to understand that going into it.

First of all, a movie trailer has the luxury of using edited footage of characters, scenes, and plot directly from the movie. It is promoting the visual and audible aspects of a movie. The equivalent for book trailers would be to show photos of the pages of your book. In order for the book trailer to have the characters come alive on the screen, you will have to pay actors to perform sections of selected scenes.

This is the reason 90% of all book trailers are boring. Music. Panning photos. Text on the screen. That's about the extent of the production. It's almost like a template where you can generically plug in information. Most do not even bother using a narrator.

It's true, a book trailer makes a great addition to your

website homepage, and can be used on your Amazon author page and to create excitement about your book on Facebook, Twitter, YouTube, and Pinterest. However, if it is a boring video, it is a boring video! And your book trailer does not have to be anything like all the others you see. Just as your book should not be like all others on the market.

I want you to understand that the concept of book trailers are meant for one thing only. And that is to drive sales. So, let's look at ways to improve the experience so you can improve the bottom line.

If getting a professional book trailer is not in your budget, then you need to know a few things when attempting to produce it yourself.

Storyboard your message

Just as your book tells a story, so should your book trailer. This very short story should introduce your book with a hook and tease your viewer with a provocative ending or question. Remember, your trailer should have a beginning, middle, and end. This is the outline of what you want to shoot.

Keep it short

One minute and fifteen seconds is generally the ideal length. Remember, people have short attention spans and their time has become their most valuable asset. Reward them for clicking on your video with a short, entertaining teaser for your new book.

End with book-specific graphics and info

End your trailer with a shot of your book cover and an

AVAILABLE NOW tag. Or, if you're using your book trailer to drive pre-orders, your tag should say "pre-order now." Regardless, the most important thing is to include specific information where the viewer can purchase the book. If possible, incorporate a hyperlink along with the video. Make it as convenient for the viewer as possible to find more information that can lead them to clicking the BUY button.

Continuity

Echo the same elements used in your book description, ending with an emotional hook or question. What hook will pique the interest of the potential reader to get more details about the book? A non-fiction book about retirement might end with "Will you outlast your money?" A dystopian novel trailer might end with "What if the only family you ever knew was a lie?"

Use high quality elements

Use professional stock footage and stock music from paid or royalty-free web sites. Montages of stills can be effective, too. Photo and video stock sites such as iStockphoto.com and depositphotos.com are good, inexpensive resources.

Voiceover talent.

Unless you are an experienced voiceover artist and you have a recording studio, use a professional. While you may be tempted to do the voiceover yourself because you are on a budget, using a professional can make the difference between a professional-looking (and sounding) trailer and one that looks amateurish.

Again, I highly recommend John DeVincent. John has been in the radio industry for years, and has served as creative director for some very large broadcast companies. You will get the highest of quality with a unique voice with John, and you will get what you ask for in the time you need it.

His email is john@johndevincent.com and his website is www.johndevincent.com. Tell him Michael Knost sent you. He's a great guy, and he is a writer, too, so, he knows where you are coming from.

Formatting

Know the various aspect ratios and preferred file formats for the sites where you will upload your trailer. This takes a little research to find the ideal file formats for most viewers. You can host your video trailer on YouTube or Vimeo and embed it on your website if you've created it with the proper aspects. The goal is to make sure that wherever you share your new book trailer, it will play at full size without being cut off or stretched to distortion. You'll want it to be an HD quality video file in 1280 x 720 resolution for best viewing on all screens.

Audio.

Good quality sound can make the difference in a book trailer. In addition to a professional voiceover narration, any music or sound effects need to be professionally added for best results, and a good sound design and engineer will use music and sound to enhance the story of your trailer message. Music sites such as freeplaymusic.com and incompetech.com are great resources for royalty-free music and more.

Put a plan into place.

Create a marketing plan for your book trailer just as you would for your book, and plan to share it on all of your social sites, your website, your author support groups, and as a link in your email signature. Social media platforms increasingly reward visual content above status-only updates. Using book trailers in your social marketing can create an emotional connection to you and your book, attracting new friends, fans, followers, subscribers, and with your professional presentation.

Getting your book trailer professionally produced would be ideal. And there are many options and companies available. I would suggest you work with a company with experience in producing book trailers. A generic video production team is not a bad selection, but if they are not experienced with book trailers then you are not getting your money's worth. Let's face it, you are paying for professional production, but you are also paying for experience...or should be.

Costs for production will vary, and most companies will have varying package levels starting from $600 and going into the thousands, each package including specific elements and range. Personally, I use aaabooktrailers.com because they are inexpensive and offer high quality and convenient turnaround times.

KISS AND MAKE UP: HOW TO FIND A BOOK PUBLICIST YOU'LL LOVE

Consider this a guest blog kind of feature. I wanted to write something on the subject of author/book publicists, and decided to ask my long-time friend Burke Allen to cover the bases for me. Burke and I go way back to middle school (or what was then called junior high) and graduated together. Burke started working in radio a few years before I even considered it, and was crucial in helping me improve my on-air skills. He was also a great resource when I began work as program director and general manager of stations.

Burke is now the Washington, DC based head of Allen Media Strategies, and currently works with authors and celebrities such a Homer Hickum (October Sky, Rocket Boys) and America's Got Talent winner Landau Eugene Murphy, Jr.

So, here's what Burke had to say:

There's a great true story about the rock band KISS in their early days that my pal Larry Harris once told me. It's also detailed in Larry's excellent book about his days as VP of record label Casablanca back in the 1970s called ...AND PARTY EVERY DAY.

It was 1973 and the wannabe stars in the fledging band KISS needed to do something ... anything ... to set themselves apart from every other longhaired rock n' roll band trying to make it in the ultra competitive music business. So, when they finally scored a showcase with Larry's fledging record label (Casablanca) in a New York City ballet studio of all places, there were less than a dozen people in the room to watch this totally unknown band try out for the label. With a huge sound and light system big enough to fill an auditorium, not a ballet dance studio, the small audience included only KISS managers, the drummer's wife, the sound man, a few hangers on, and my friend Larry, who was one of two folks from the record label -- the other was his cousin, soon to be legendary Casablanca head Neil Bogart.

When KISS tromped out in their white powder and greasepaint Kabuki makeup, leather pants and jackets and platform heels, Larry remembers them as "seven foot tall monsters in eight inch heels that took the stage. They had a way-too-loud sound system that caused my ears to literally ring for the next two days. Neil and I were sitting there in metal folding chairs, and I couldn't take my eyes off the spectacle. This is way before the fire, the blood, the drum risers, the costumes, but these guys demanded your attention, and there was no way you could walk away from them feeling apathetic. Love 'em or hate 'em, you were going to have a strong reaction."

For KISS, their days as four anonymous guys playing in jeans and tee-shirts in dive bars all over New York's outer boroughs were about to be behind them. It had come down to doing whatever they could to get the world to pay attention to them. Their plan worked; Casablanca Records signed KISS later that week, and the rest is platinum selling rock and roll history.

It's a lot like that in book publicity. You can write the best book ever, but if you don't take extraordinary steps to get potential readers to notice it, your book will languish with the millions of others out there that get read by a handful of friends and family members. And maybe that's all you want. But if not, if you want the best, you've got the best (sorry, it's a KISS reference), I've put together a handy checklist of what to look for when you're considering hiring a publicist to help you get the word out on your book.

By the way, you may be saying to yourself "I can do this myself ... I don't need a publicist", and that may very well be true. Every so often, we run across authors who have the skills to go it alone. Usually though, authors prefer to spend their time actually ... writing. What a concept! So, they or their publishers come to firms like mine to do what we do, so that the writers can do what they do.

So, here they are, Allen Media Strategies Top Five Tips On Hiring A Publicist Who Will Fight For You and Your Book. These are in no particular order, because they're all equally important.

Make a List, and Check It Twice

Set up a phone call (or even better a video conference or in-person meeting) to make sure you're comfortable with the publicist. You need a bit of a connection and a touch of chemistry for this relationship to work, just like any relationship. One "chemistry" buzz kill can be specialization; in today's world, some publicists specialize in only one thing, like doctors. If they only do conservative media, and Republicans make you break out in hives, keep looking.

If they only book radio interviews, and online and social

media is a hot button for your book campaign, say sayonara. See if you can get a feel for their attention to detail; I'm not talking about asking for reports of everyone they contact and how many times they've followed up; you shouldn't care about failed attempts, you should care about their wins. Instead, find out if they can do the basics, like spell your name right, get your time zone vs. the media outlets time zone down correctly, and proof read their releases before they hit the "send" button.

Are they capable of staying on top of your daily calendar, so they don't try to book you when you're unavailable? Trust your gut here. And don't be afraid to bring a list of questions you want to ask; there's no such thing as a stupid question when it comes to spending your hard earned bucks on PR, so if the publicist gets bent out of shape when you ask questions, as Bill Engvall says "here's your sign." Move on.

Check Their Track Record

Any quality publicist should be able to supply references for several current or former clients that you can speak with, and list a handful of campaigns they've worked on before. When you do contact them, ask the publicist's clients how accessible he or she was for them; did they return phone calls and emails promptly? Was there a good balance between youthful enthusiasm and grizzled veteran experience? Did the publicist offer sage advice and guidance?

Most authors tend to think of publicists as the person who scores the big interview, but the really good ones are also strategy consultants who will help you boost your brand and your book sales over the long term. Did the author you've contacted for a reference ever do a media tour with the publicist, and if so, how did the publicist perform in person with the media pro? Were they willing to shift tactics and alter strategy during the campaign if a course correction was agreed upon? Have they achieved the kind of results you're looking for? I don't mean all their authors get on every major media outlet no matter who they are or what their book is about.

Manage Your Own Expectations

Sure, you think your book is the bee's knees. All your close pals and relatives have told you so, so it must be true. That doesn't mean that it's an automatic slam-dunk in generating PR. Does the book have a broad enough appeal that media outlets will want to feature it somehow? Are there multiple hooks that tie into the news cycle in some way? If not, it's going to be tough (but not impossible) to gain mainstream traction.

Fortunately, in today's world, there are media targets (many online) for all kinds of special interests, and chances are your book will be a good fit for some blog, podcast, or other exposure outlet. Just a few years ago, book publicity meant newspaper reviews and NPR. Today, not only have things changed dramatically, they're constantly evolving. People and outlets come and go every day, and you can't possibly keep up on all that change, but a great publicist can.

Don't Let The Tail Wag The Dog

Great PR is a collaborative effort. You're going to need to lean on the publicist's expertise on what's achievable, where the media targets are and are not, and how to translate your expertise and book topics into possible exposure. But having said that, you shouldn't do anything you're not comfortable with. Don't think you're ready to go toe-to-toe with Howard Stern? Break out in hives at the thought of doing a TV interview? Tell the publicist BEFORE you engage them.

The before part is crucial, because nothing will build a wall between you and your PR firm quicker than if they spend dozens of hours on pursuing and then finally landing an interview for you, which you then decline … for any reason. You've not only wasted their time, you've burned their media contact. So, get a game plan together before the pitching begins. Remember, you've hired a publicist to make you busier, so you need to make your book PR a priority and do everything you can to be available for every reasonable opportunity.

In fact, with a bit of media training to get you more comfortable, you should be able to handle Howard and lots more (and most really savvy publicists can help you with media training, or refer you to someone who can help). Don't want to do media with a left or right political lean because you don't want to get sucked into a partisan conversation? Then, you're leaving a ton of great exposure opportunities on the table. Instead of taking a pass, consider getting trained on how to redirect the conversation with bridging language ie. "Well, Rush, I can't tell you that, but what I can tell you is …. " Politicians do it all the time, and you're campaigning for your book, so you can, too.

Don't Base Your PR Campaign on Direct ROI (Return On Investment)

We'd love to tell you that when it comes to book sales, "interview A led to a direct sales of B," but it just doesn't work that way. There are a gazillion variables that influence book sales in relation to publicity; how often was the title of the book mentioned in the interview, did the outlet link properly to your book sales page, were you a compelling interview subject while subtly selling the book, was the media outlet congruent with potential readers, are you getting buried by a huge story in the news cycle, is there any paid marketing for the book ... I could go on and on and on here.

Many times, book sales gain momentum from great word of mouth, which most realistic publicists will tell you is still the best PR (of course, that word of mouth often starts with an interview, a book review, or some other book exposure). Besides, most authors don't have access to precise sales analytics, and that goes for everyone from #1 bestsellers with big New York publishers to self-published authors who only utilize online sellers like Amazon and B&N.com. The bottom line is that you can't always figure out how or why someone decided to visit an online retailer or his or her local bookstore (if they even have one still) to buy your book.

So, now that you've got my top five tips, get out there and get your book noticed. And take solace in the fact that you don't have to wear greasepaint, breathe fire and wear leather S&M outfits with platform boots to get exposure. Not that there's anything wrong with that. In fact, it could be fun!

Burke Allen is the Washington, DC based head of Allen Media Strategies. Burke brings three decades of media experience to his team's work with authors, speakers and entertainers from New York Times best sellers to self published and independent authors. You can find out more about the firm at www.allenmediastrategies.com. He first saw KISS in 1979.

ALWAYS LOOK FOR A CONNECTION.

I am always surprised by how many writers overlook extraordinary opportunities to promote their book and their brand. I believe it often comes down to thinking too small. And it's sad, because all too often it could take something as simple as a phone call to trigger a next-level event.

For instance, my latest novel, *Return of the Mothman* is a huge hit in the state of West Virginia, where sightings of the creature are well known. And there seems to be a plethora of Mothman merchandise everywhere one looks. There is even a Mothman Festival every September in Point Pleasant, West Virginia.

Just recently, I learned there is a brewery in our state that produces a Mothman IPA beer. The cans and bottles are marketed nicely with a rendition of the creature with the glowing red eyes and everything. Obviously, there is a connection with my book, so, I called the brewery and spoke to the marketing director. I explained who I was, and the Mothman books that I have written, including the latest novel. I mentioned that it would be fun to create some kind of an event where we put the two together -- a book signing and beer event. Well, the marketing director loved this idea, and has now begun preparations and planning for something along those lines.

Michael Knost

Now, I mentioned this a few times, but I think it is important to bring up again. Last year, I contacted my local Cinema complex regarding their flashback Friday movie nights. During the month of October, the cinemas have showings classic horror movies for a cheaper ticket price and usually pack the place. So, I wondered if they would be willing to show the old Richard Gere movie *Mothman Prophecies* and allow me to do a book signing during the showings. They loved the idea. So, I set up a table, and sold a ton of Mothman books before and after each showing of the movie.

Now, none of these events would have happened had I not recognized the connections, and contacted the entities involved. When it comes to connecting with events or businesses, that have some kind of connection with you or the content of your book or books, when you approach them, you want to make sure that you do not come across is a parasite. You do not want them to think you are going to latch onto them and suck their blood without doing something to bring benefit of some sort to them.

Therefore, it is always good to explain what you can do to bring more people to their business -- especially a number of customers they may not see all the time. Or maybe you can explain how much publicity you are going to bring to the table. You could talk about your plans of contacting the media and scheduling interviews in order to promote the event, or convincing the television news stations to send reporters to cover everything that is going on. This will put you in a more favorable light with the owner of the business as they see this as a benefit to them as well. Always consider yourself a partner with anyone, or any entity, that you work with or around in this manner.

Think about it, if you were to go into business with

a partner, you would expect both individuals to bring something to the table for the partnership. One may bring financing and resources, and the other may bring expertise or talent. But, the partnership works because each individual needs the other in order for the business to work. And you have to think along the same lines when you are dealing with a connecting business or entity.

Let's take a look at some examples of looking for the connection. Let's say you wrote a book on the subject of pumpkins, and you discovered that in Circleville, Ohio, the town puts on a pumpkin event. Seriously, this thing is enormous. And anything you can think of that is related to pumpkins you will find there. And I mean anything. Would you not think it a great idea to set up a booth and sell your book? Even if you have to pay for a table to be there, you know beyond a shadow of doubt, this is a no-brainer.

Let's say you wrote a book about Halloween. It seems almost every year a month or two before October comes around, an enormous store emerges in or around larger malls that focuses on everything Halloween. We are talking costumes, decorations, and gags. This would be a perfect opportunity for you to partner with this particular business and focus on getting as many people to come to see both you and the store together.

Or maybe you have written a fictional love story that is set during the time when women played baseball while the men were overseas fighting in the war. If you have seen the movie *A League of Their Own*, then you will know what I am talking about. Now, if you discover that there will be a traveling museum of items from the women's league during that era, it would be a great opportunity to attach yourself and your book to that event in some way.

Never think small. And another thing, never say no for

someone else. I remember selling radio advertising when I was younger and had several packages to offer. I'll never forget the time I was visiting the owner of a dealership about doing a small sponsorship for the local high school football game we aired on the weekends. It was a small package that didn't cost a lot of money as the owner always balked at big packages.

After I explained the high school football package, he said, "Why is the station not airing the West Virginia University games this year?"

"Oh, we will be airing those games as we have for years," I said.

His eyebrows quickly came down over the bridge of his nose. "Well, why are you not pitching that package to me? You know I am a WVU graduate!"

"I'm sorry," I said. "I was afraid the package was too much for your budget."

His face reddened. "Why don't you let me say no? Okay? Don't say no for me!"

I use that advice in everything now. Sure, the brewery could have said no when I called to inquire about putting together and event with their beer and my books. Yes, the cinema owners could have said no to bringing the old Mothman Prophesies to the theater and allow me to sell books before, during, and after the shows. However, on each account, had I not made the calls, I would have been saying NO for them. And guess what? They both said yes. Had I not called I would have been saying NO for them when they would not have.

Don't be afraid to ask. Don't be afraid to try. It will NEVER hurt even if they say no. Don't say NO for them! At least give them the courtesy of saying it. And, remember, if you don't ask, you will never know the truth.

INTERVIEW WITH LUCY A. SNYDER

Lucy A. Snyder is a four-time Bram Stoker Award-winning writer and the author of the novels Spellbent, Shotgun Sorceress, and Switchblade Goddess. She also authored the nonfiction book Shooting Yourself in the Head For Fun and Profit: A Writer's Survival Guide and the story collections Soft Apocalypses, Orchid Carousals, Sparks and Shadows, Chimeric Machines, and Installing Linux on a Dead Badger.

Her writing has been translated into French, Russian, and Japanese editions and has appeared in publications such as Apex Magazine, Nightmare Magazine, Pseudopod, Strange Horizons, Weird Tales, Steampunk World, In the Court of the Yellow King, Shadows Over Main Street, Qualia Nous, The Library of the Dead, and Best Horror of the Year, Vol. 5.

She lives in Columbus, Ohio and is a mentor in Seton Hill University's MFA program in Writing Popular Fiction. She also writes a column for Horror World. You can learn more about her at www.lucysnyder.com and you can follow her on Twitter at @LucyASnyder.

MICHAEL KNOST: What tips can you offer to create and grow a solid readership base?

LUCY A. SNYDER: First of all, write the best work you possibly can. Always look for ways to improve the books and stories you're presenting your readers. All the marketing in the world won't help you if you aren't offering work that readers will enjoy. Write well, write as much as you can, and get your work out there. Many authors earn their readers one at a time. Social media can help, but don't be a jerk. Some people will follow combative authors to watch the constant train wrecks, but that kind of followership seldom translates into book sales.

KNOST: Do you think awards can help an author with regard to marketing?

SNYDER: Oh, definitely, but the marketing value rises with the prestige of the award. My work got tremendous exposure after winning the Bram Stoker Award; probably you could multiply that exposure times 10,000 for a Pulitzer winner! Readers will buy a book that's won an award they recognize as being a genuine mark of quality; a smaller number will give a book a try if it's an award they don't recognize. I think "awards" that authors pay for and which only function as marketing tools don't help much.

KNOST: What precautions do you take to protect your name brand?

SNYDER: I usually write under my real name, so my "brand" is me at my writerly best. My brand is my personal reputation, so I always try to write my best work and conduct myself as a professional. I don't engage with negative reviewers; that just never works out well.

KNOST: How important is face-to-face networking?

SNYDER: It is hugely important. My first four book deals happened because I knew editors who were familiar with (and liked) my work; I first met all of them at conventions and other events where I'd talked to them and found out what they were looking for. Most of the short story sales I've made the past few years have been to invitation-only anthologies, and a fair number of those invitations came after I talked to the editors or publishers at conventions.

When I was finishing my novel Spellbent, I knew from watching others' experiences that I wanted a good agent shopping it around for me. So I started asking author acquaintances if their agents were currently taking new clients; I quickly got a referral to my current agent. I never once cracked a copy of Writer's Market or Literary Market Place. My speedy, successful agent hunt was pure networking.

Tomorrow, I'm leaving for AnimeKon in Barbados. I'll be their featured author guest, which means that the convention paid for my flight and hotel room. To Barbados. How did I get this extremely sweet gig? Networking.

Networking is crucial in making deals of all kinds, but all the schmoozing in the world is meaningless if you can't back it up with a solid publications history and a demonstrated ability to produce good work on deadline.

KNOST: What book marketing tactic do you believe to be least effective?

SNYDER: Tying advance reading copies of your books to

bricks and throwing them through strangers' windows just doesn't work very well. Neither does painting "Buy my book, you jerks!" on your naked butt and streaking down a major thoroughfare at high noon. I mean, I've heard these things don't work. I haven't tried them. Honest.

KNOST: In your opinion, how important are book readings when it comes to marketing and success?

SNYDER: If you're a good story performer and you're reading to a large group, you can end up selling a lot of copies to impressed audience members. The problem is that many authors are not good readers and readings at bookstores and conventions are often poorly-attended unless you're already a well-known author (or reading with one who is). But I think readings are worth doing, partly because they're a staple at conferences and being willing to read makes it more likely that you'll be asked to participate. So, it's worth practicing and becoming a good reader.

CUSTOMER RETENTION

It's obvious to think of your readers as customers. But, you should also think of the people who hire you to speak, teach, or attend events, as customers. I'm talking about libraries, conventions, writer retreats, and workshops.

Customer retention is important in order for you to continue your business of writing, speaking, teaching, etc. One of the main reasons is you want readers of your first book to read your second, and third, and so forth. You also want the library that paid you to come speak last year to ask you to come again this year or next year. Customer retention can make you or break you in any business, and that includes ours.

I am reminded of the time my wife and I moved to a nice neighborhood in North Carolina. The house was beautiful, but the yard was in terrible shape. So, we decided to set out plants and flowers, trees, mulch, and a few tacky decorations to drive the neighbors crazy.

So, we headed to the Home Depot to get started. The problem was we had no idea what we were doing. We quickly learned there are many choices and decisions to make. However, the biggest choice, which has nothing to do with geography, is whether we wanted Perennials or Annuals. How were we supposed to know? We knew there were flowers that die each season and others that always return, but we didn't know what they were called or how to control this miracle of nature.

Since we never did this before, we pleaded ignorance and asked for help. What we learned was that Perennials come back every year and Annuals last only for one season and never come back. Sounds pretty simple, doesn't it? Well, not quite. There's a price to pay for the yearly return of these flowering marvels. While Annuals don't need much tending to, aside from routine watering, it seems that Perennials need a bit more caring. Perennials need to be fed, they need to be weeded, they need insecticides, they need pruning, and they need continuous attention to ensure their healthy return and growth each and every year.

At this point I began to think about work and my customers as I managed a few radio stations at the time and saw a striking resemblance. It occurred to me that customers are like flowers and you can treat them either like Perennials or Annuals. Sure, you can acquire a new customer, sell them what they need, and then move on to the next prospective buyer. These customers will blossom nicely for a while with their new product or service. You can even use them as a showcase, or reference account, to show other prospects what a good job you do for your customers.

However, without continuous care and attention, they will eventually die off, not as a business entity or individual of course, but as a customer of yours. You will lose them as a client. Like an Annual, their flowers will fall off and they will wither away and never return. With the costs of acquiring new customers being 7 to 10 times higher than selling to your existing customers, according to studies, why would any business not want to do everything they could to retain their existing customer base? This, of course, requires businesses to treat their customers like Perennials, not Annuals.

With constant care and attention, your customers will remain loyal and dedicated to your business. They'll keep coming back year after year flowering you with more business. It's not sufficient, either, to simply care for your customers "just enough" to keep them from complaining. If you barely water and feed your Perennials just enough for them to flower and return each year, you will more than likely only get marginal results. The flowers will be sparse and lackluster.

Likewise, if you simply keep your customers satisfied, you may also get marginal results. Today, customers are so used to poor service and performance that they have learned to accept mediocrity as the norm. It's a sad state of affairs, but an unfortunate reality in today's business world. As a result, when customers receive minimum service and attention, they are satisfied only for the simple reason that they were not treated poorly or negatively.

This sort of treatment will never yield a fully blossoming relationship, nor loyalty to your company. Marginal service will yield marginal results. Consequently, loyalty and commitment to your business will suffer. Your clients will migrate to another competitor as soon as they see a better offer. What many businesses don't realize is that the relationship begins, not ends, after the sale is made. Once the sale is made, this is your time to shine and show the customer what you are really all about.

What is needed is exceptional service – above and beyond what is expected. Your customers should be so happy with your service, support, and attention that they actually tell other people about their experience with your business. Librarians telling other librarians what a great speaker you are, and how you go the extra mile.

If you take really good care of your Perennials, they will come back year after year in full bloom and continue to grow and prosper. Your customers will do the same. Exactly how should you care for your customers?

Feeding

Just like Perennials, you must feed your customers. Feed them with attention. Show them you care. Feed them information about you or your books or your services, and any other information that can help their business grow. Even though they are already a client of yours doesn't mean they know everything going on in your business. If you won an award, expanded your business, delivered a new product or service, or changed in any way, let them know. This shows them that you are not stagnating and will continue to be there for them in the future. It will also help their business as well.

Weeding

Don't let your customers get choked by problems. Just like clearing deadly weeds from around your flowers, help solve problems for your customers. Your sales ordering and delivery processes should be problem free. If they aren't, fix them. If there's a problem with your product or service that is affecting your customer, do everything possible to resolve it. The best way to know if there are problems is to ask. Don't wait for your customers to call you with problems. Call them and ask how things are going and be prepared to jump to the rescue if there are problems. Just like Perennials, weed before they start to die.

Spraying

You don't want those pesky bugs destroying your Perennials. Likewise, you don't want those pesky competitors destroying the relationship you have with your customers. So, prevent that from happening by ensuring you have a healthy, positive relationship with your client so when a competitor comes calling, your client isn't prone to listen. We all know someone who pays a little more or travels a little further to deal with a business simply because they like the relationship they have with them. It isn't always about money, but it's almost always about the relationship. Keep the bugs, and competitors, away.

Pruning

Perennials need to be pruned, or cut back, to prevent wild growth. Wild growth is not just unsightly, but it is bad for the plant, since the food and water cannot reasonably satisfy the requirements of an overgrown plant. The result could be weak and sickly looking flowers. Businesses need to prune their customers as well or else they will grow larger than their capacity to service their clients successfully. Don't be afraid to walk away from business. If it is too large for you to handle, don't let greed cause you to take on too much and get over your head. It will negatively affect the relationships with your existing customers. Don't be afraid to fire your customers. If they are causing you to move into a direction that is not the focus of your business or that is not in line with your business plan, tell them so they can either work within your business strategy or move on to another vendor. Controlled grow is good growth whether you are a business or a Perennial.

Caring

Perennials don't grow healthy all by themselves. The previous tips show there is a lot that needs to be done to ensure healthy plants. This means you have to care for them and about them. Same with your customers. In addition to the previous tips, general caring is in order. Stay in touch and don't be a stranger. You sold them your product; therefore, it is your responsibility to make sure it is indeed what they needed, that it solved the problem in which it was intended, and that they know you honestly care about the success and growth of their business. Caring means going beyond a client-vendor relationship. It's about a Partnership. You take care of them, and they'll take care of you – year after year.

So now that we have a beautiful floral garden in our yard, we expect to see it grow and flourish every year with proper care and feeding. Your customer base is the same way. They are your garden and you have to take proper care so you can enjoy them year after year.

This is called "Customer Lifecycle Management." You market to suspects, sell to prospects, and support customers. As you ensure your customers are happy, Raving Fans, you continue to market and sell to them. This is more cost-effective and efficient for you, and better for your clients since they continue to benefit from what you have to offer and from your lifetime relationship. Now, it's off to the garden to do some weeding.

ABOUT THE AUTHOR

Michael Knost is an author, editor, and columnist of science fiction, fantasy, horror, and supernatural thrillers. He has written in various genres and helmed several anthologies. His *Writers Workshop of Horror* (Woodland Press) won the 2009 Bram Stoker Award® for superior achievement in nonfiction. His critically acclaimed *Writers Workshop of Science Fiction & Fantasy* (Seventh Star Press) is an Amazon #1 bestseller. His recent novel, *Return of the Mothman* (Woodland Press) was a finalist for the Bram Stoker Award® for superior achievement in first novel.

Michael is currently the Mentorship Program chair for the Horror Writers Association and has taught writing classes and workshops at several colleges, conventions, and online. He resides in Chapmanville, West Virginia with his wife, daughter, and a zombie goldfish. To find out more, visit www. MichaelKnost.com.

Check out the following pages
to see more from

SEVENTH STAR PRESS

All Seventh Star Press titles available
in print and an array of specially priced
eBook formats.

Visit www.seventhstarpress.com for
further information

Connect with Seventh Star Press at
www.seventhstarpress.com
seventhstarpress.blogspot.com
www.facebook.com/seventhstarpress
www.twitter.com/7thstarpress

Transcend Reality!

Stephen Zimmer Brings You a New Sword and Sorcery
Heroine with the Heart of a Lion!

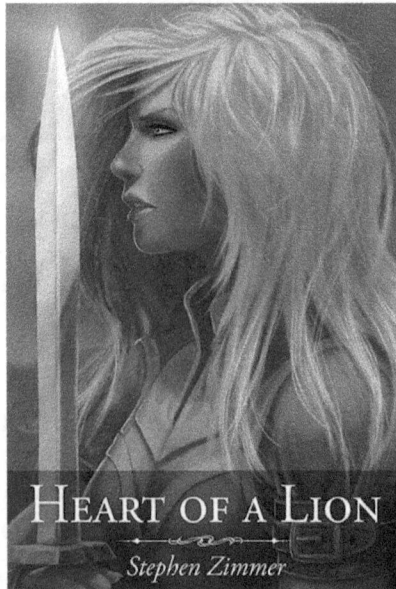

HEART OF A LION
Stephen Zimmer

Softcover ISBN: 978-1-941706-21-3
eBook ISBN: 978-1-941706-23-7

Rayden Valkyrie. She walks alone, serving no king, emperor, or master. Forged in the fires of tragedy, she has no place she truly calls home.

A deadly warrior wielding both blade and axe, Rayden is the bane of the wicked and corrupt. To many others, she is the most loyal and dedicated of friends, an ally who is unyielding in the most dangerous of circumstances.

Both friends and enemies alike swiftly learn that the people of the far southern lands spoke truly. Rayden Valkyrie has the heart of a lion.

Heart of a Lion is Book One of the Dark Sun Dawn Trilogy.

Also from Bram Stoker Award-winning Michael Knost!

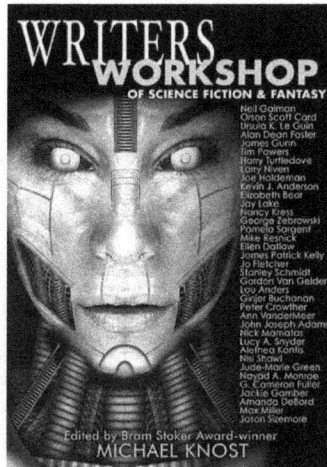

Softcover ISBN:
978-1-937929-61-9
eBook ISBN:
978-1-937929-62-6

Writers Workshop of Science Fiction and Fantasy is a collection of essays and interviews by and with many of the movers-and-shakers in the industry. Each contributor covers the specific element of craft he or she excels in. Expect to find varying perspectives and viewpoints, which is why you many find differing opinions on any particular subject.

This is, after all, a collection of advice from professional storytellers. And no two writers have made it to the stage via the same journey-each has made his or her own path to success. And that's one of the strengths of this book. The reader is afforded the luxury of discovering various approaches and then is allowed to choose what works best for him or her.

Featuring essays and interviews with:
Neil Gaiman, Orson Scott Card, Ursula K. Le Guin, Alan Dean Foster, James Gunn, Tim Powers, Harry Turtledove, Larry Niven, Joe Haldeman, Kevin J. Anderson, Elizabeth Bear, Jay Lake, Nancy Kress, George Zebrowski, Pamela Sargent, Mike Resnick, Ellen Datlow, James Patrick Kelly, Jo Fletcher, Stanley Schmidt, Gordon Van Gelder, Lou Anders, Peter Crowther, Ann VanderMeer, Joh Joseph Adams, Nick Mamatas, Lucy A. Snyder, Alethea Kontis, Nisi Shawl, Jude-Marie Green, Nayad A. Monroe, G. Cameron Fuller, Jackie Gamber, Amanda DeBord, Max Miller, Jason Sizemore.

Now Available from Seventh Star Press,
the horror stylings of
Michael West!

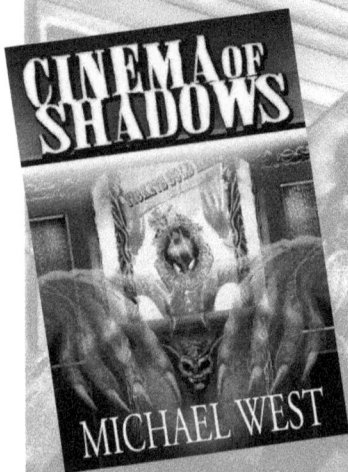

Trade Paperback ISBN: 9780983740209
eBook ISBN: 9780983740216

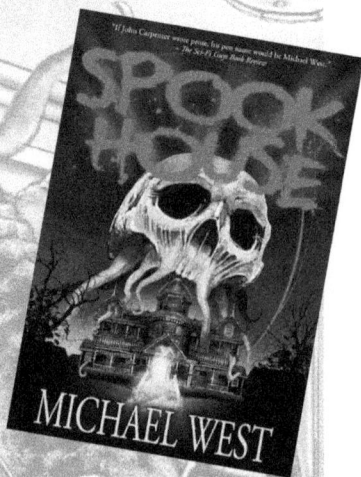

Trade Paperback ISBN: 9781937929718
eBook ISBN: 9781937929725

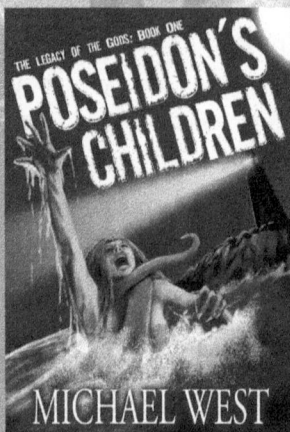

Trade Paperback ISBN: 9781937929954
eBook ISBN:9781937929831

Trade Paperback ISBN: 978-1-937929-18-3
eBook ISBN: 978-1-937929-19-0

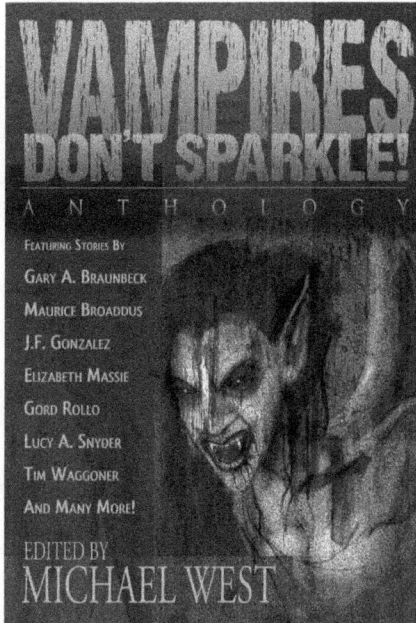

eBook ISBN: 978-1-937929-69-5
Softcover ISBN: 978-1-937929-60-2

Vampires Don't Sparkle! poses the question: What would you do if you had unlimited power and eternal life?

Would you...go back to high school? Attend the same classes year after year, going through the pomp and circumstance of one graduation after another, until you found the perfect date to take to prom? Would you...spend your days moping and brooding, finding your only joy in a game of baseball on a stormy day? Or would you...do something else?

The authors of this collection have a few ideas; some fanciful, some humorous, and some as dark as an endless night.

Join us, and discover what it truly means to be "vampyre."

Shadows Over Somerset from Bob Freeman!

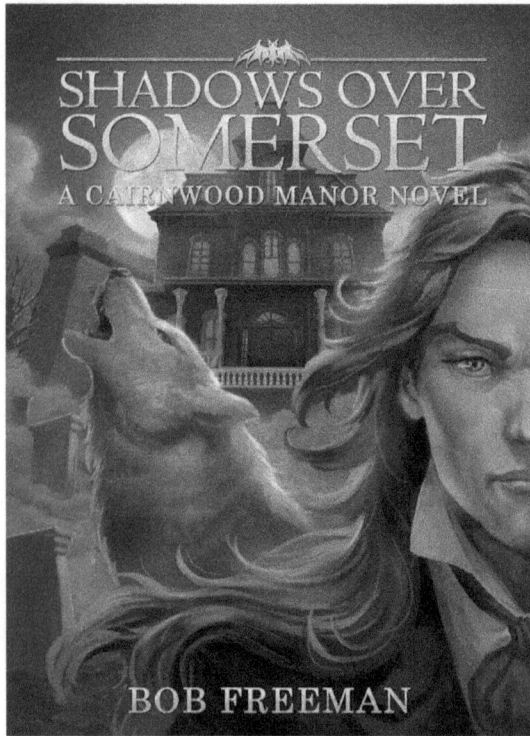

Softcover: 978-1-941706-11-4
eBook: 978-1-941706-12-1

Michael Somers is brought to Cairnwood, an isolated manor in rural Indiana, to sit at the deathbed of a grandfather he never knew existed. He soon finds himself drawn into a strange and esoteric world filled with werewolves, vampires, witches... and a family curse that dates back to fourteenth century Scotland. In the sleepy little town of Somerset, an ancient evil awakens, hungering for blood and vengeance... and if Michael is to survive he must face his inner demons and embrace his family's dark past. Shadows Over Somerset is the first Cairnwood Manor Novel.

Urban Fantasy from John F. Allen!
Meet Ivory Blaque!

Softcover: 978-1-937929-16-9
eBook: 978-1-937929-17-6

In The God Killers, the first book of The God Killers Legacy, former professional art thief Ivory Blaque is hired to procure a pair of antique pistols and gets much more than she bargained for when several attempts are made on her life.

Her client turns out to be a shadowy government agent who reveals that she is descended from a race of immortals, and that the pistols are linked to her unique heritage and the special psychic gifts she possesses. He uses the memory of her father to guilt her into working for him.

Ivory eventually gives in to his request, and in return, he presents her with her father's journal, which was written in an unbreakable code. Bishop believes that she is the only one capable of breaking the code and unlocking the plans of the vampire hierarchy. But when the city's top vampire is a sexy incubus with an attraction for her and she's assigned a hot new lycan enforcer to protect her, she finds herself caught between two sets of rock hard abs.

To regain her autonomy, clear her name, unlock the secrets of her past, and protect the lives of those closest to her, Ivory must play along with the forces trying to manipulate her. Ivory's life is rapidly spiraling out of control and headed for an explosive conclusion which she just might not survive.

16 Tales of the Paranormal and Ghostly from editors Alexander S. Brown and J.L. Mulvihill!

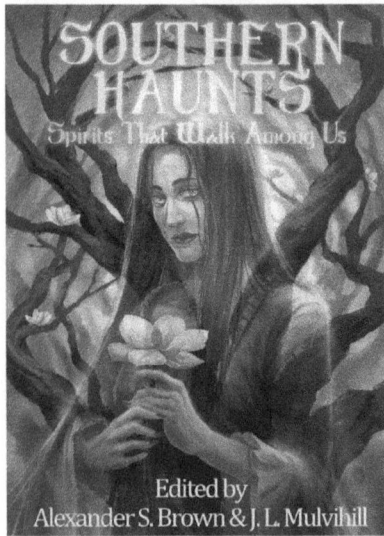

Edited by
Alexander S. Brown & J. L. Mulvihill

eBook ISBN: 978-1-937929-14-5
Softcover ISBN: 978-1-937929-12-1

From the shadowed realms of the paranormal comes 16 chilling tales that dwell in the South and South West. From 16 authors, learn of haunted homes, buildings, landmarks and roads where restless entities from beyond the grave desire acknowledgement amongst the living. Become acquainted with the aftermath of an eclipse that awakens the dead in a Memphis cemetery, see what horrors dwell in the woods at Hell's Gate, learn the dark secrets of Sidney's Cotton, and dare to travel down Ghost Road. These and many other tales are sure to keep you awake as you are introduced to what makes the South and South West so unique.... History and GHOSTS!!!!! So, sit back, dim the lights and prepare yourself to face the spirits that walk among us.

Paranormal-laced Horror from Crymsyn Hart!

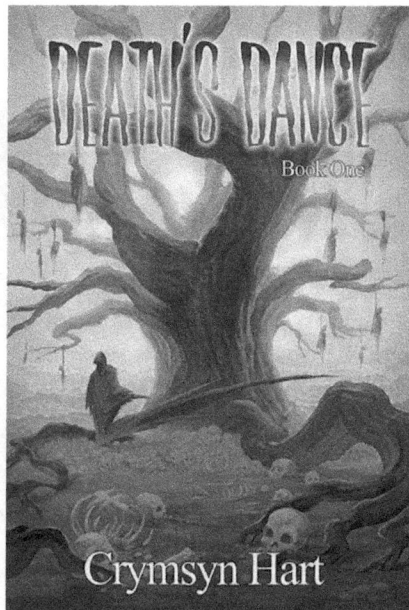

Softcover: 978-1-941706-13-8
eBook: 978-1-941706-14-5

Being a psychic, you would think talking to the dead was a walk in the park. However, it's not always that simple. The hooded specter haunting me is one I've been dreaming about since I was a kid. One day, he appeared in my bedroom mirror. Good. Evil. I don't know what his true intentions are.

Enter Jackson, ghost hunting show host extraordinaire, and my ex, to save me from the big bad ghost.

From there…well…it's been a world wind of complications. My house burnt down. I'm being stalked by an ancient evil and gotten myself back into the world of being a ghost hunting psychic. Jackson dragged me, along with a few other psychics, to a ghost town wiped off the map called Death's Dance.

From there things went from bad to worse.

Death's Dance is Book One of the Deathly Encounters Series

Appalachian Gothic! Jason Sizemore's Irredeemable!
18 Tales of dark fantasy, science fiction, and horror

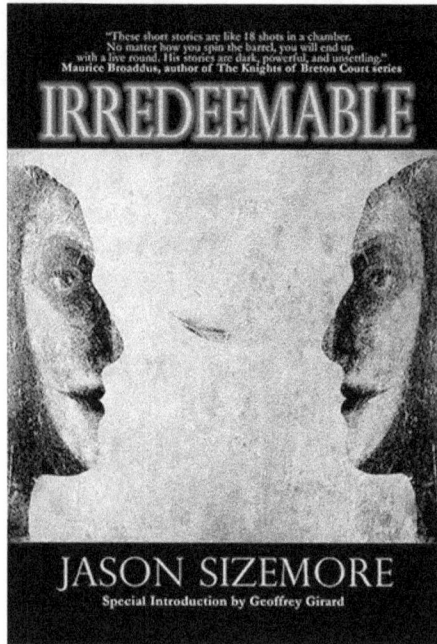

"These short stories are like 18 shots in a chamber.
No matter how you spin the barrel, you will end up
with a live round. His stories are dark, powerful, and unsettling."
Maurice Broaddus, author of The Knights of Breton Court series

IRREDEEMABLE

JASON SIZEMORE
Special Introduction by Geoffrey Girard

Softcover: 978-1-937929-59-6
eBook: 978-1-937929-68-8

Flowing like mists and shadows through the Appalachian Mountains come 18 tales from the mind of Jason Sizemore. Weaving together elements of southern gothic, science fiction, fantasy, horror, the supernatural, and much more, this diverse collection of short stories brings you an array of characters who must face accountability, responsibility, and, more ominously, retribution.

Whether it is Jack Taylor readying for a macabre, terrifying night in "The Sleeping Quartet," the Wayne brothers and mischief gone badly awry in "Pranks," the title character in "The Dead and Metty Crawford," or the church congregation and their welcoming of a special visitor in "Yellow Warblers," Irredeemable introduces you to a range of ordinary people who come face to face with extraordinary situations.

Whether the undead, aliens, ghosts, or killers of the yakuza, dangers of all kinds lurk within the darkness for those who dare tread upon its ground. Hop aboard and settle in, Irredeemable will take you on an unforgettable ride along a dark speculative fiction road.

Post-apocalyptic, zombie-infested military thriller from
Peter Welmerink!

Softcover ISBN: 978-1-941706-03-9
eBook ISBN: 978-1-941706-02-2

The HURON, a 72-ton heavy transport vehicle and an army of four; tracked, racked and ready to roll, to serve and protect the walled metropolis of Grand Rapids-both her living and her undead. Captain Jacob Billet and his crew patrol the byways, ready for trouble. William Lettner, the North Shore Coalition High Commissioner, has enemies from the mainland to the lakeshore and needs to be covertly transported home after his helicopter is shot down en route to Grand Rapids. He has no love for a city that give unliving civilians the right to survive. Lettner's venomous outbursts assaults Billet and his crew along every mile travelled as they are assigned to safely bring him through the treacherous landscape outside the city back to his hometown. To complete their mission, the HURON and her crew will have to face domesticated zombies and the feral undead; marauders holding strategic chokepoints hostage; barricaded villages fighting for survival, and a group of geneticists who've lost control of one of their monstrous experiments. The crew will need to stay strong and trust one another in order to finish the mission and bring their "precious" cargo home, even knowing, all the while, the terrible deeds Lettner has done. Travelling through West Michigan was never so dangerous. Transport is the first book in the Transport series!

From the Mind of Acclaimed Horror Author Brick Marlin
Comes a Shadow Out of the Sky!

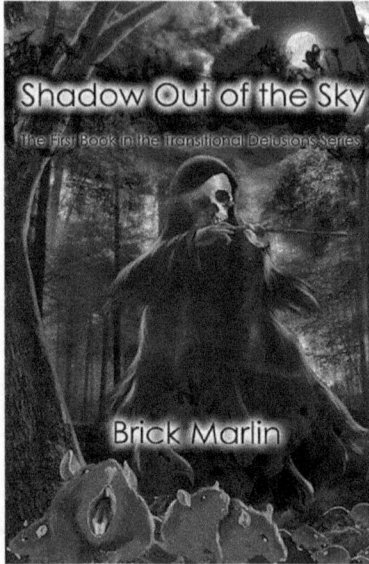

eBook ISBN: 978-1-941706-17-6
Softcover ISBN: 978-1-941706-20-6

A scarecrow crucified on a wooden cross made from a pair of two-by-fours sits in a field of corn, placed there to frighten away birds and protect the crops. Under its straw hat large buttons pose as its eyes, placed there by child's fingers, view something sinister in the grave sky, appearing in front of the full moon.

Twisting, it forms into a sleek black mass, peering down upon the town of Woodbury. Four demons called The Reckoning has pulled this shadow, this urban legend from the past, out of an unmarked grave to bring terror across the planet, shoving it toward an apocalypse.

Now it cuts through the air, as if it were opening wounds in flesh, peering down at the first house that it hovers over...

Shadow Out of the Sky is Book One of the Transitional Delusions Series

www.ingramcontent.com/pod-product-compliance
Lightning Source LLC
Chambersburg PA
CBHW022015090426
42739CB00006BA/142